ONCE UPON A HILL

GLENN PATTERSON is the author of seven novels, the most recent of which is *The Third Party*. A collection of his journalism was published as *Lapsed Protestant* in 2006. His television work includes documentaries and series for Channel 4, BBC4, BBCNI, UTV, RTE and Granada. He lives in Belfast and teaches creative writing at Queen's University.

BY THE SAME AUTHOR

Burning Your Own
Fat Lad
Black Night at Big Thunder Mountain
The International
Number 5
That Which Was
Lapsed Protestant
The Third Party

For my girls

Contents

Now that they're dead, nobody can know.

Philip Roth, *The Human Stain*

The two of you up a tree, k-i-s-s-i-n-g,
First comes love, then comes marriage,
Then comes a baby in a carriage.

Playground taunt

The town of Lisburn, in the county of Antrim, is built upon a hill of no great elevation.

Henry Bayly, *Topographical & Historical Account of Lisburn* (1834)

Prologue

In the autumn of 1989, having exhausted all the options, I moved to Lisburn, eight miles south of Belfast, and took a flat on Bachelors Walk, fifty yards from the train station, and a two-minute walk in the opposite direction from the centre of town. I thought I had Lisburn pretty well worked out, well enough not to want to get any deeper into its backwaters than fifty yards from the train station. A minute and a half into the walk up the town, left at the bottom of Bachelors Walk, I passed 9 Antrim Street, Apollo Window Blinds in 1989, for ever to me the house where my father had grown up. (The Apollo makeover had risen no higher than the sign above the front door. I recognised the green paint on the first-floor window frames. I could have sworn I recognised the blinds, and they certainly weren't Apollo's.) I had visited my grand-parents here at least once a week throughout my childhood and with my three older brothers had tried to find ways to keep myself amused in a house without television, in which even the radio seemed never to be switched on. In my memory we spent a lot of time around the vending machines outside Mrs Thompson's sweet shop, a dozen doors down the street, putting pennies in the slots and trying to get enough of a grip on the worn metal knobs on the sides to claim our packets of Beech-Nut and Arrowmint chewing gum. I remembered too, from far, far back, my confusion, verging on terror, on seeing Davy Jones, at under four foot Ireland's smallest man, getting out of his custom-built red sports car across the road from number 9. And I remembered, following the introduction of troops to Northern Ireland in August 1969 (I had just turned eight), watching from the doorstep as heavy-duty armoured cars came down the street on their way to Thiepval Barracks – army HQ – half a mile up the Magheralave Road past the train station.*

Twenty years on from that summer, my grandparents were both long dead, but I still had an aunt, my father's sister Eileen, living in the town. Now a widow in her mid-seventies, Eileen had lived all of her own married life in Antrim Street, directly opposite my grandparents for much of it, and still walked most days the three-quarters of a mile into the town centre from her new home on the Old Warren housing estate, if for no other reason than to replenish the stock of cakes and scones with which you were endlessly plied whenever you called out to see her. Eileen was a fixture on the

---

* Davy Jones's red sports car is on permanent display in the Ulster Folk and Transport Museum at Cultra. Armoured cars can now be booked for stag and hen nights. I am told they were particularly popular for a time in west Belfast, although their day may have come and gone. The 'Hire Engine' is today's party vehicle of choice. Nothing like a big hose and a hard hat to get you in the mood.

I hope you are OK, by the way, getting down here with me. You will be in very good company, if that's any incentive: Charlie Chaplin, James Cagney, the Prince and Princess of Wales; although sometimes there will just be us, and the name of a book I have read.

concourse of Bow Street Mall, built on the site of the alleys and entries that had once packed the right angle between Antrim Street and Chapel Hill, or at least built on the site of Crazy Prices, which was the first supermarket worthy of the name I was ever in, and which had already while I was still a child made inroads into the old housing stock.

Crazy Prices was now Stewart's Supermarket, the mall's anchor tenant. I would see Eileen two or three times a week on a bench close to the Stewart's entrance, midway between HMV and Winemark, although to be honest I tried to avoid her (it was not hard: she was usually talking), for whenever she did see me Eileen would insist on giving me money, just as she had in the days when I was running down Antrim Street to the chewing-gum machine. Now instead of pennies it was a pound, fifty pee, whatever she had at the bottom of her purse. Her son Jim was often with her. If there was nothing at all at the bottom of the purse he would get a dunt in the ribs. *Look in your pockets*, the dunt said, while Eileen's mouth distracted me with enquiries after my parents' health, my brothers' children, my own well-being up there in that flat all by myself.

I was twenty-eight years old. I had published my first novel, *Burning Your Own*, the year before. I was in Lisburn at the behest of the Arts Council of Northern Ireland, which had appointed me writer-in-the-community for the town: in Lisburn despite initial hopes that 'in-the-community' would not necessarily imply 'in-residence'. I held a weekly surgery at the local arts centre (there were some very, very sick stories out there, let me tell you), visited secondary schools and libraries in neighbouring towns, organised literary events in the bar across the road from my flat, the Robin's Nest. I was far from broke and far from invisible. You could not fault her heart, but really, in more ways than one, the last thing I needed was my Aunt Eileen pressing money into my hand in the centre of Bow Street Mall.

If I had not intended being in Lisburn in the autumn of 1989 I had not intended either being anywhere like as close to Belfast. I had been living in England for the previous seven years, the last two in Manchester. Manchester had just gone Mad. Happy Mondays, Hacienda Mad. Manchester had swagger; Manchester had baggy style. The T-shirts in Afflecks Palace on Oldham Street boasted 'On the Seventh Day God Created Manchester' and 'Manchester, North of England'. So of course within a matter of weeks T-shirts began to appear on the other side of the Pennines: 'Leeds, North of Manchester'.

Manchester was a great place to be twenty-eight in, if not always at that time a great place in which to get any work done. Even without the madness I had been having difficulty getting going on my second novel, set like the first in Northern Ireland, but unlike the first set in the present day. I had come home at the turn of the year in the hope that being here would help me see what the novel was Really About, which proved to be Not an Awful Lot. I binned the first draft and started again. (Who am I kidding 'binned'? I boxed it up and left it in my parents' attic with the A-Level French essays I had never thrown away.) I was just persuading myself that the novel had begun to take root when the Arts Council post came up. It was a three-year contract, more than enough time for me to complete the novel, with as many weekends as I could manage besides back in Manchester.

As it turned out I finished the novel (and soon after the job) in a little under two years. I called it *Fat Lad*, a mnemonic I had been taught in primary school for the six counties of Northern Ireland: Fermanagh, Antrim, Tyrone, Londonderry, Armagh and Down. We had very short memories in my primary school. Very short and (*London*derry) very Protestant.

The novel tells of a man in his twenties returning to Belfast from an unspecified city in the north of England (although not Leeds; definitely not Leeds), trying to come to terms with his family and by extension with his upbringing in Northern Ireland, with the place itself: hence the title. Despite the fact that I had returned from a city in the north of England to write it, and had had to get used again to daily contact with my own family, Drew Linden, the central character, was as close as it was possible to get to pure invention. Actually in my mind he looked a lot like a boy named Tom for whom a girl I had gone out with at school was always threatening to dump me. Analyse that.

I did not know then that in my Aunt Eileen, Antrim Street, the Robin's Nest come to that, there was a family story to rival anything I could cook up in my imagination. I did not know that when, a couple of years after leaving Lisburn, I found myself in another writer-in-residence post, at University College Cork – found myself in love, the course of my life about to be re-plotted – I had actually moved closer to the heart of that story, closer even to the scene of one of its key events.

I came back to Belfast finally in the spring of 1994, pausing only long enough in Manchester en route from Cork to pack up my belongings. Ali, who I had met in a bar on Cork's MacCurtain Street (she was coming off duty as a singing telegram), came with me. We had been born five days short of eleven years apart. We remarked on it the night we met then never mentioned it again. We had been baptised into different faiths. I do not remember us ever mentioning it at all before we decided to move to Belfast.

Within days of our setting up home there together, the UVF murdered a young Catholic taxi driver in Carrickfergus, just north of Belfast. His Protestant girlfriend spoke on the evening news of her grief and outrage: her boyfriend's killers were evil people, the scum of the earth. I sat on the floor in front of our portable TV, amid the boxes still to be unpacked, and cried and cried and cried, for him, for her, for the two of us. The next day the UVF ordered the woman's entire family to get out of the country.* A month later another Catholic man was murdered in the Rathcoole estate, halfway to Carrick, while his Protestant girlfriend begged for his life.

It often seemed as though the bigots here reserved a special hatred for mixed relationships, perhaps because mixed relationships gave the lie to the idea that there existed two distinct peoples in Northern Ireland, although you cannot discount the possibility that, in a society where housing had become more segregated with every passing year, the internal borders more impenetrable, such relationships simply offered the gunmen some very convenient targets.

On the final day of August 1994 the Provisional IRA announced a 'complete cessation of military operations' (military operations? Don't start me) and was followed into ceasefire six weeks and another pointless murder later by the UVF and the several other loyalist terror groups.

Ali and I were married the following May in the registry office on Grattan Street, behind Cork Courthouse, despite a

---

* Her family were 'permitted' to return eventually, which was big of the UVF; she has never come back.

late attempt by Ali's grandmother – 'Gibby' to her grand-children – to talk her into the chapel of the university where I had been in residence and from which Ali had recently graduated.

I was a Protestant? That could be 'fixed'.

She was over eighty by the time I got to know her, Gibby, tiny and powdery and shaken by Parkinson's, but – something in her eye – she did give you the impression that she had the know-how, and the connections, to fix just about anything.

The registry office might not have been the most inspiring of venues (it had the unused look of the Complaints Room in the old Carlsberg lager ad; the roof behind the table at which we exchanged rings leaked), but it was a reaffirmation to each other that religion had no place in our lives. We would choose for ourselves the words by which we were defined.

When we got back from honeymoon a couple of weeks later, my parents arranged a dinner in a hotel outside Belfast for family and friends who had not been in Cork for the wedding. (The registry office sat about twelve at a squeeze.) My Aunt Eileen did not come. She had recently been diagnosed with Alzheimer's. One of the first signs had been the cupboard full of uneaten cakes and scones, which she had continued to buy like there was no tomorrow, even though she had not got through yesterday's, or the day before's, or even, by the looks of some of the cakes, the week's or the month's before that. Later that year she was admitted to a specialist dementia unit at the Lagan Valley Hospital and that, I am ashamed to say, was the last I ever saw of her. Ashamed and not a little chagrined. She might have told me much that I needed to know. If only I had known in time that I needed to know it.

What follows is as much an account of how I became aware of what it was I did need to know, as it is a chronology of the events themselves. At times I felt as though I was inching back along a tunnel lit only by the match-flare of some chance remark, a snippet, a newspaper spill, and then all of a sudden the flame would gutter and I would find myself plastered against the tunnel wall as the past hurtled by, its carriages brightly lit, its passengers jabbering away nineteen to the dozen, on the wrong side of the glass, just this side of blur.

I will try not to let them hurtle. I will try not to let them slip back into the dark.

Names and Dates (1)

There were always going to be problems with dates. The registration of births, deaths and marriages in Ireland did not begin until 1864, twenty-seven years later than in the rest of the United Kingdom, as it then was, or as it still is, minus twenty-six of the thirty-two counties of Ireland. That transition – from 'Ireland' to 'Northern Ireland and the Republic of Ireland', by way of 'Northern Ireland and the Free State', and 'Northern Ireland and Éire' – created additional problems. There are no electoral registers here for the years 1916–1921, that is from the time of the Easter Rising to the end of the War of Independence, otherwise known as the Anglo-Irish War, also known as the Tan War. Many other records were lost in the burning of the Four Courts in Dublin during the Irish Civil War that followed.*

And then, more prosaically, previous generations were not as scrupulous as our own about birthdays and anniversaries.

* The Tan War like the Rising and the Civil War is all going a bit sepia now that there are no more than a handful of survivors, although it was only within my lifetime, 1966, that an Irish premier was elected who had not taken up arms against the British, or members of the Opposition.

Not as scrupulous or not as in thrall to Hallmark. The year before my Aunt Eileen's fiftieth birthday my father asked his parents about their golden wedding anniversary, surely approaching. My grandfather told him, somewhat abruptly, that they did not go in for all that, which my father, who had not had a birthday card, much less an anniversary card, from his parents in his life, accepted readily enough.

My grandfather, all the same, was never without a pocket diary. Top of my pile of grandfather-memories is him sitting in an armchair in the living room of my parents' house, mid-1970s, the *Sunday Post* open on his lap, stopping in the turning of a page and dipping into his jacket for his diary and a pen to make a note of some reader's tip.

In the next memory down he sits in the same chair, drumming his fingers on the arm, not impatiently (my grandfather was one of the most self-contained, and self-controlled, men you could ever meet), but simply keeping time with a tune in his head: a march, more than likely, possibly a hymn. *Drum, drum, drum* . . . Dip into the pocket where the diary was kept; make another note.

I have one of his diaries beside me as I write, A7 size, week-to-view, a royal-blue cover with the Faith Mission crest – a cross, girdled by a crown – and the year 1970 in gold. Inside is a very useful chart to enable you to calculate the day of the week for any date from 1900 to 1987 inclusive, which means it stops well short of the day, or night, I came by the diary, although I can tell you it was 1st February 2005, a Tuesday. Manchester United walloped Arsenal 4–2 at Highbury, which would have been memorable enough, and my father and his two surviving brothers arrived at my house bearing the box-files and zip-folders of the family archive. That I had first talked about writing a book six years earlier, only to be told there was some 'unhappiness' at the prospect from those selfsame brothers, hardly for the time being mattered, any more than it did that Manchester United did not go on from their victory over Arsenal to win the League: I mean, 4–2, at Highbury. The handover was more symbolic than practical. We already knew there were gaps in the archive. This was my permission to write into them. Eileen's death the previous year had been a sort of catalyst, for me as well as for my father and my uncles. For me before them: I had not waited for the permission to start. Still it was good to have it. It was good to have the Faith Mission diary.

I have turned to the day-finding chart more than once to pin a definite date on some of the events of this story, although of even greater use might have been a key to the organisation of the diary itself. The first entry of the year looks as though it was indeed copied out of the *Sunday Post*: 'Muir (herbalist), 24 Nicolson Street, Edinburgh 8. "Capital" foot ease ointment. 3/8 post free.'*

A page has been torn out between the week beginning Sunday 4th January and the week ending Saturday 17th. (In Faith Mission diaries the week always begins with a Sunday.) The days that remain are covered in calculations and decimal conversions, all scribbled over with the exception of a sum subtracting 1879 from 1967 to leave 88. An age at death, I fear. The entry for Epiphany is my Uncle Edmund's Co-op number. Over the page, under Monday 19th, my grandfather

---

* A story in the *Scotsman* in July 2007 claimed that Muir had been the model for an irascible Scots chef, called Crock, developed by Muir's grandson, Canadian comic Dave Thomas. Crock was in turn the model for Grounds-keeper Willie in *The Simpsons*. Capital!

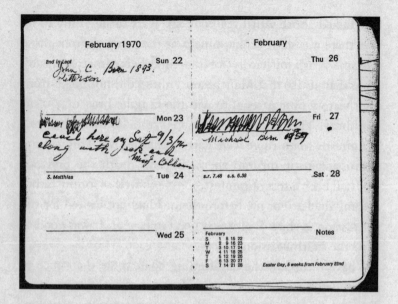

has written the name of my other uncle: 'David C. Born
1926', a Tuesday, according to the chart. On the page facing,
under Thursday 22nd (full moon), is a name and address:
John Wylie, 4 S____ Gardens, Bangor.

A month on, Sunday 22nd February carries the legend, 'John
C. Patterson born 1893'. That, although you would never guess
it from the formal tone, is him: my grandfather. The C is for
Clements, as it is in David C. (his mother's middle name).

It is the entry for the day after his birthday where things
really start to go awry. Under Monday 23rd is written, 'Cecil
here on Sat 9/3/74 along with Jack* and Miss F. Calhoun.'
Thereafter the years 1971, −2, −3 and −4 are as likely to
appear as the 1970 advertised on the cover. Thus, Friday 8th
May: 'Ears syringed 1970. Syringed again 17/7/73.'

* His second son, my late Uncle Jackie, born the year after David.

Thursday 16th April records that W. Russell cleaned the chimney for twelve shillings and sixpence, but that the price had gone up to fourteen-and-six when he came back again on 2nd February 1971 and up again, to sixteen shillings, on his return in November 1972.* A summer holiday as a widower – 'At Portstewart with Jack, 17th–24th August 1973' – is recorded on 20th August, a little under four weeks before the date of a day trip made three years earlier, before his bereavement: Tuesday 15th September 1970 (Battle of Britain day), 'At Ballyhalbert caravan-site with Jack and Molly and Phares [all scored out] Mother and I.'

This is my grandmother's second mention. The first is on her birthday, 26th July, a Sunday in 1970. Here she is Catherine. The year of her birth, originally in blue, has been gone over in black. It looks as though 1896 has been amended to 1894, more likely than not after her death, midway between the day trip to Ballyhalbert caravan-site and the holiday in Portstewart, on 8th February 1972. The birth date has been amended again at the back of the diary, in the pages left blank for notes, where my grandfather has a comprehensive list of births and deaths. (I am there, missing an 'n', next to my 9/8/61.) My grandmother's death is recorded in the same black pen as has earlier changed 6 to 4: 'Catherine (my dear wife) died 8/2/72.' Below that is the date of her mother's death, 8/2/37: exactly thirty-five years before. Now my grandmother is Kitty, as stark a contrast to 'Mother' as it is possible to imagine.

* The W was for William, although he more often got Billy. He cleaned my parents' chimney too, arriving by bicycle with his brushes slung in a bag from the crossbar; didn't say a lot, but whistled as he went about his keyhole-surgeon's task, a near-silent whistle that was more like a perpetual clearing of dust from the lungs.

[A photograph of a handwritten diary page listing family names and dates, including entries such as "William E Patterson Born 5/4/1879", "David H.P. DIED 26/8/70", "Pharos (Fred) DIED 1890", "John C.", "Catherine DIED 8/2 26/11/1893", "Eileen 32/9/1894", "David C 9/1/1915", "John E 26/4/1922", "Pharos 26/6/1929", "Wm Edmund 19/3/32", "Sharon E. 3/1/52", "Michael David 29/1/57", "Brian 8/2/55", "Paul 8/4/56", "Kevin 18/10/58", "Glen 7/8/61", "Catherine Ann Cathy 13/4/59", "Terence 16/13/61", "James Smylie died 1/1/72 18/5/61", "Eleanor (Ella) 17/12/1961", "James (Jim) 18/9/63", "Norma 29/8/68", "Nessie 19/4/74", "Molly 26/8/77", "Isobel 15/7/77"; and on the right side: "Emma Patterson Born 1884", "Agnes Edith D 1/3/1911 1886", "Emma Harriet D 9/2/1849 ..12/1/88", "Father BORN 1860 died 12/12/1894", "Mother born 21/8 18.../1925", "William Edw BORN 1864 24/2/61", "David died 26/8/70", "Harry Porter died 8/2/72", "Catherine (my dear wife) 8/2/72", "Dora died 8/1/94", "Fred", "Kitty's mother died 8/12/3.")]

And he had other names for her, which are not in the diary. 'The Greatest Little Woman in Lisburn', was one. She, in return, used to point across the room at him and tell people, 'That is the best man that ever lived.'

The names were not simply interchangeable. Each one had its precise time, its proper place. My Uncle David, introducing his parents to a work colleague, made the mistake of calling his mother Kitty.

'*Catherine*,' my grandfather corrected him. 'It's Catherine.'

Sometimes he called her, as her sisters and brothers called her, Kate, which is the name I choose to use, the name that fits best with his. Not John Samuel Clements, as he was christened in full, or even John C. as he preferred to sign himself, but Jack, as he was almost always known: Jack and Kate, equal length and weight.

The memories of my grandfather sitting in my parents' house

with the *Sunday Post* are from after my grandmother's death. Her death is the reason he is there at all, digesting, culling ads for 'capital' foot-ease ointment. If I try to imagine the two of them together it is the kitchen of 9 Antrim Street I see. The kitchen is pretty much the whole of the downstairs of 9 Antrim Street. To the right, beneath the window as you come in off the street, is a table covered with an oilcloth, a chair beyond it where my grandmother sits. To the left, just past the door leading on to the stairs, is a dark and elaborate dresser affair (dark despite the mirror at its centre), which seems to have come from an altogether grander house. Even its name – the chiffonier – is an awkward fit. Facing this, and much more in keeping, is a Modern Mistress range (at least it was modern in 1948 when it replaced the open fire), with a hinged bracket and hotplate for the kettle and another for baking the soda bread that my grandmother keeps in one of the chiffonier's drawers. My grandfather's chair is off to the side, between the range and the curtain into the scullery. On the wall behind him, above the wireless set, hangs a photographic portrait of his father as a young man. Upstairs, although I have no recollection of it, is a companion-photograph of his mother in – the kind of thing you would definitely remember if you had seen it – a triangular frame.

From its position on the mantelpiece between the Staffordshire china dogs, a clock ticks stagily.

My grandfather is wearing a grandfather shirt – what else? – and two pieces of a three-piece suit. (The jacket will be hooked over one of the chiffonier's little ornamental urns.) He needs the waistcoat for his watch and chain. My grandmother is mostly middle and wears a cardigan over a floral print pinafore. She has her hat on: a small, black hat, where 'small' and 'black' are the sum total of what you might describe as

style. Maybe she has just come in. She likes to stand at the
front door greeting passers-by. If she does not know you by
name you will get a simple 'Hello, Man', or 'Hello, Woman'.
Sometimes you will get an apple or an orange to go with it.

For many years my Uncle David had a wholesale grocery
business in Belfast and Newtownards and would bring boxes
of groceries in the car with him whenever he called, things
his parents might not think to, or be able to, buy themselves:
tins of salmon and what have you. These too Kate regularly
gave away to visitors and strangers alike.

My mother, when she and my father had just started going
out together in the early 1950s, was always sent home with
something. One night when there was nothing else in the
house (a busy day on the doorstep, obviously) my grandmother gave her an egg. My mother held it in her hand the
ten and more miles and two bus journeys to her home at the
top of Belfast's Woodvale Road. Her own parents, Annie and
Billy Murphy, were a generation younger than her future in-
laws and were just about, in the early 1950s, to embark on a

new life in Canada. They were, to me, who only met them long after the transplant was complete, slacks and perms to Jack and Kate's waistcoats and hatpins, barbecues to their tea and barmbrack and strangers brought in for a 'hate' by the fire.

Jack could sometimes be sparing with the coal. Kate would push him out of the way and shovel it on.

'You never know who is going to call,' she would say, then, when someone did happen by, 'See, didn't I tell you?'*

Kate was, my mother tells me, 'a nice wee woman' then adds, without malice, 'a naïve wee woman in some ways'. My Aunt Eileen's daughter Ella, who spent large parts of her Antrim Street childhood across the road in number 9, calls her 'a wee Earth Mother'.

She was not tall, my grandmother. You will have gathered that.

She had grown as far up as she was ever going to get in 44 Chapel Hill, just round the corner from Antrim Street, but in those days close to the very edge of town – the edge of the whole workaday world, the way she talked about it. She regaled her children with stories of the fairies at the bottom of her garden: 'a great big garden', she assured my mother, although then again she would tell anyone who would listen that she had been born on a cold, cold winter's morning, snow lying thick on the ground, which even allowing for the vicissitudes of our North Atlantic climate is a fanciful

* The coalman, in fact, was one of the regular beneficiaries of her hospitality. He would carry the bags of coal in by the front door, through the kitchen, the scullery, and out into the yard, and by the time the last bag was emptied Kate would have his dinner on the table. At least his was a familiar face. My father says it was not unusual to come home from work and find someone sitting there eating who you had never clapped eyes on before.

description of late July. (I have seen forty-seven of them; I know all the variations.)

The 1911 census lists fifty-two out-offices and farmstead-ings on Chapel Hill, including eleven stables, two coach-houses, three cow-houses, three piggeries, three fowl-houses, three turf-houses, one boiling house, three sheds, five work-shops, six stores, and two forges. None of these is associated with number 44, although the general farmyard air might account for my grandmother's confusion, late in her life, about the nature of our pet hamster.* It must have been explained to her that the trembling, musty-smelling creature presented to her in my cupped hands was a bit like a guinea pig, but somewhere along the way the 'guinea' had fallen off.

Whenever we visited after that she never failed to ask, 'How is the wee pig keeping?'

I rack my brains, but those are the only words I can with certainty remember my grandmother saying to me, smiling out from under her little black hat.

'How is the wee pig?'

---

* This would have been Hammy I, who my mother brought home one day in a shoebox from a trip to the local Spar. A neighbour had found him in her garden, escaped from who-knows-what out-office or farmsteading. A knot of women (I spotted a typo in the first draft: 'a know of women'; I was half inclined to leave it, but in this instance they really were more knot than know) was standing at the fence, looking at him, when my mother passed. She was the only one who would pick him up. On his second Christmas with us Hammy I – at that stage still plain 'Hammy' – swallowed a fir-tree needle while out for a run around the living room, after which my brothers and I had Hammy II and two years later Hammy III and two years later girlfriends, whereupon the empty cage was left to rust in the garage.

Names and Dates (2)

The Pattersons, my father used to love to tell us, were thrown out of Scotland for stealing sheep. His cousin, who did extensive work on the family tree, back when the family-tree industry was still in the nursery, records that Pattersons were among the 10,000 lowland Scots who crossed to north-east County Down in 1606, a good three years ahead of the Plantation proper, under the leadership of Sir James Hamilton, a sometime Latin school proprietor, Fellow of Trinity College Dublin, government agent, and master of political intrigue: 'chancer', I believe, is the technical term. The story of how Hamilton and a rival chancer/Trinity Fellow, Hugh Montgomery, between them duped and bullied the ruling Con O'Neill out of his 'Claneboye' lands is as hilarious as it is heartbreaking (Con died penniless), but suffice here to say that, like many another story since, it all began with a party at which Con ran out of wine.

The son of one of those first, freelance colonists described them as 'scum' – I repeat: the *son* – 'scum, who from debt, or breaking or fleeing from justice, or seeking shelter, came hither, hoping to be without fear of man's justice, in a land where there was nothing, or but little yet, of the fear of God'.*

My father and his cousin shared the same forename: Phares. Two syllables, the first vowel an 'eh', not an 'ah'. Cousin Phares's father, Jack's third-eldest brother, was also a Phares, although he went all his life by Fred, which given the misspellings and mispronunciations that my father has been subject to down the years was probably a wise move. It is a name that recurs so often in the family as to seem a part of its DNA. (Family-tree DNA did not exist when Cousin Phares was doing his work. He died a stranger to the PC.) There are Johns, Davids, Williams, Samuels, Edmunds too, but there are Johns, Davids, Williams, Samuels, even Edmunds, aplenty throughout counties Down and Antrim. Any time you encounter a Phares Patterson, however, it is a fairly safe bet that you are encountering one of my own father's line. My mother, whose head had once been turned by my father's teenage nickname, the Big Wheel (another kind of Ferris altogether), used to tell us that his given name was a 'begat'. Matthew 1:3, 'And Judas begat Phares and Zara of Thamar; and Phares begat Esrom; and Esrom begat Aram.'

Matthew, however, scarcely does justice to the name (also spelt Pharez and Perez, just as it was, speculatively, in some

* My father's cousin was more interested in the source of his ancestors than the source of his quotations; I have no idea where he found this. Sources for Sir James Hamilton are even more numerous than his previous careers. The ones I have drawn on are *Two Centuries of Life in Down: 1600–1800*, by John Stevenson, first published in 1920, reprinted in 1990 by White Row Press, and *The History of the Town of Belfast, With an Accurate Account of its Former and Present State* (1823), by George Benn, who sees in the demise of Conn O'Neil [sic] 'as striking an example of the mutability of human affairs as many which have been held up for the wonder and instruction of mankind' (p. 269).

of the cards strung out every Christmas along our living-room wall), or to the story that gives rise to it. For the full-on Phares effect you have to go right back to the book of Genesis, chapter thirty-eight. Tamar was married to Er, eldest son of Judah. God slew Er for unspecified wickedness *in his sight*. Judah gave Tamar to Er's brother Onan, who of course reacted by spilling his seed. God slew Onan too. (God was in his free-slaying phase, not yet being a father himself. I mean, *Er*, God, what could be more human?) Judah told Tamar to go back to her father's house until his third son, Shelah, was old enough for her, although secretly Judah, twice bitten, thrice shy, had no intention of letting Tamar near another of his children. So Shelah grew and Tamar waited, and waited, and heard no more about it. Then Judah's wife Shuah died, of non-wickedness-related causes, I am happy to report, and Judah, after a suitable period of mourning, set off for the hills to shear his sheep. Tamar got wind of his going out. She disguised herself as a harlot and hung around at the side of the road Judah had to travel, then – never was word more appropriate – waylaid him. Or, as the King James version so beautifully puts it, '[Judah] came in unto her'; price, one goat.

The fruit of this roadside union was twins.

And it came to pass, when she travailed, that the one put out his hand: and the midwife took and bound upon his hand a scarlet thread, saying, This came out first./ And it came to pass, as he drew back his hand, that, behold, his brother came out: and she said, How hast thou broken forth? *this* breach *be* upon thee: therefore his name was called Pharez./ And

afterwards came out his brother, that had the scarlet thread
upon his hand: and his name was called Zarah. (Genesis
38:28–30)

What has always fascinated me about this – fascinated me even
more than my father's name originating in the same racy
narrative as Onan (you took your raciness where you could find
it when I was a kid) – is that the story of the twins' birth is cited by
many as the real source of the Red Hand symbol. Certainly it has
features in common with the more widely known version, in
which two competitors for the title of King are racing to reach the
Ulster shore, when in desperation the one who is lagging behind
lops off his hand with a sword and hurls it on to the beach, thus
establishing a pattern for northern Irish history: we will hold the
land even if we have to mutilate ourselves in the process.*

One particularly bonkers – so of course, down the years,
surprisingly popular – theory is that Zarah's ancestors,
disinherited by Phares's 'bursting forth' (a literal translation
of the name), wandered the earth for generations before
winding up in Ireland.

I can only imagine how their descendants must have felt
several score of begats later, seeing a load of Phareses land in
from Scotland with the chancer Hamilton.

Quick, grab the sheep! Grab the scarlet thread!

There is a significant concentration of Pattersons in the
townlands around the County Down village of Annahilt,

---

* This pattern, as everyone knows, was torn up in St Andrews on 13th October
2006. Nowadays the loser of the race would cheerfully cut off his own hand too
to make sure the winner did not leave himself at a disadvantage in the long
term. After which a choir of schoolchildren would sing a song of peace and love
and the healing of wounds; as why shouldn't they.

especially in Cargycreevy, on the Old Ballynahinch Road, about four miles south of Lisburn. Tombstones in Cargy-creevy Presbyterian Church yard throw up a Pharis and a Ferris (dead long before the big wheel had currency) and so many Pattersons besides that for a moment on entering you wonder whether the cemetery hasn't benefited from some early form of corporate sponsorship. I could ask for no clearer proof that all that will be left of me too one day will be a name carved in stoned, fading.

In the neighbouring parish of Magheradrool, meanwhile, a Pharis Patterson appears in the tithe book of 1834 for the townland of Ballykine Lower. According to my father's cousin this land had then only recently been mapped out and it seems likely that Pharis had moved there as a young married man. He has a little over five acres, at a tithe of nine shillings and threepence halfpenny. (Never mind the amounts, that little word 'tithe' is a measure of the gulf between us.) He appears again – as Phares – in the records of First Ballynahinch Presbyterian Church at the marriage, in 1849, of his son William to Margaret Smiley of Glasdrummond. A record exists of another son, James, christened in 1844, but he and his mother Sarah, née McKelvey, are absent from the census of 1851, at which point Phares is living with William and Margaret and an infant named Mary Ann. The years in between were the famine years and although Ulster was not as gravely afflicted as the rest of the island it is possible that Sarah and James fell victim to it. (Magheradrool translates into English as 'land of difficulties'.) Then again, levels of infant mortality remained high throughout the century. Of Mary Ann there is no further trace either after the early 1850s, nor yet of the son, Sam, born to William and Margaret in 1854.

Bizarrely, and I trust coincidentally, one of the few surviving public records of Magheradrool in these years is a report on the County Down assizes of October 1853 at which the case was heard of a male child secretly buried in the parish churchyard. Indeed, the correspondent writes, for two years previously the churchyard has been a hangout for 'certain disorderly persons' who have turned it into a 'hiding place (a very aceldama) for murdered innocents and others supposed to have come to an untimely end'. The magistrate was less alarmed. The case was dismissed for lack of evidence and with a recommendation that no more bodies be exhumed in consideration of the wasted time and money.

Aceldama, like tithe, is not a word you hear a lot these days.*

William and Margaret moved for a time to a small house on land owned by Samuel Martin, where William carried on his trade as a weaver. By 1863, however, they were back on the family farm, Phares, William's father, having died in the meantime. They set about rebuilding the house, which appears to have become quite substantial, quadrupling in rateable value (at last: rates!) from five shillings to a pound. The money for these improvements probably came from Margaret, whose family held significantly more land than the Pattersons – eighty acres – and who brought to the marriage nineteen in her own name.

This money may have played a part in the advancement of Margaret and William's sole surviving child, my great-

* For Aceldama see one of the bloodier Acts of the Apostles; for Magheradrool see Ros Davies's County Down Genealogy Research website, which includes references to over seven thousand place names, and hand-drawn maps of every one of the county's several hundred townlands. And all (blow the dust off 'global village' before you pass it to me) co-ordinated from Australia.

grandfather Phares, born, according to Jack's Faith Mission diary, '1860 app.'

In fact, on his marriage to Eleanor Clements Spence of Lisnastrain, County Down, on 18th January 1878, Phares declares himself a full-age bachelor, that is, over the age of twenty-one, which implies a birth date no later than the first few weeks of 1857. Eleanor is the source of even greater confusion. The Cousin Phares family tree has her born in 1862, which would have made her barely sixteen on her wedding day, a long way off the full-age spinster of her marriage certificate. She gave her age as forty-one on 3rd April 1901 in the census of that year, but in the follow-up census of 1911 she has aged eighteen years, owning up to fifty-nine. After that the ageing process slows down again. On her death certificate, fourteen years later, she is said to be sixty-three. Consult the actual register of deaths for 1925, however, and you will find a note in the margin: 'In No. 453 for 63 years read 72 years. Corrected on 24th January 1925 by Mr _, Registrar, on production of a statutory declaration made by John C. Patterson, son of the deceased.'

Jack the inveterate amender, although whatever it was he knew in 1925 he had apparently forgotten by 1970. The entry for Eleanor's birth at the back of his diary tails off after the month: 21/8/ . . .

The missing digits – all power to the online genealogical search! Or at least to the Ulster Historical Foundation, which hosts AncestryIreland.com – are unquestionably 5 and 2. Her family too was living in Annahilt parish when she was born, in Ballylintagh, 'the townland of the flax pools'. Her father, Mitchell Spence, styled himself by turns a farmer and a weaver, like most of his neighbours in those twilight years of cottage industry. Ros Davies, the expert on County Down townlands, makes a point of saying that many Ballylintagh women spun yarn, linen and cotton. Eleanor by the time she married had become a skilled dressmaker. Her mother Margaret's maiden name, McClamond, was anglicised to give Eleanor the middle name she passed on to Jack, who in turn passed it on to his first-born son. She had two older brothers, William and John, and a younger sister, Agnes, and may also have had a not-too-distant connection to her future husband's family. In later life Eleanor was very thick, is I think the best word, with a family called Dunwoody – cousins of hers, my father and his brothers are adamant – and for a time had a niece, Isabella P. Dunwoody, lodging with her. The P according to Isabella's marriage certificate (1919; she was twenty-nine) is for Patterson and she was born in Cargycreevy.

The certificate also records that her husband was one John Horn, a customs officer from Regina, in the Canadian province of Alberta, to where she evidently returned with him after the wedding: she has no death certificate in Ireland.

From a Cargycreevy Dunwoody to a Regina Horn in one 'I do'. It is a loss, I cannot help feeling, of more than just a few syllables.

There is one other birth date, if I can call it that, that my grandfather omits from his diary, whose omission is, if anything, more perplexing than a couple of numbers from the end of his mother's. It is the date on which the Jack I knew came into being, was, to use the term preferred these days, born again. One of the biggest problems when it came to piecing this story together – bigger than all the eccentricities of chronometry, the inevitable elisions and erasures of the passing of years – was imagining that some of the events related to the same man who visited our house every Sunday after his wife died and in preparation for whose arrival my brothers and I used to have to lug the television up to one of our bedrooms so that we could watch the *Big Match* without his knowing.

My grandfather did not hold with TV on a Sunday; he did not hold with anything much beyond the *Sunday Post* and his meeting, to which my father would drive him directly after Sunday tea and from which he would collect him again a couple of hours later, often with me in the car, to drive him back to Lisburn. The meeting hall was off the city end of the Malone Road, close to Belfast's Queen's University, squeezed between tall, redbrick terraces subdivided into student flats and bedsits. I went to grammar school a little way down the road (and now that I think of it smoked up an entry in the next street), but if I ever saw the hall in daylight all the brightness has leached from my memory. Religion as my grandfather practised it was unremittingly grim to me.

He was 'saved' after attending an evangelist mission by William – 'WP' – Nicholson. Nicholson, a native of Bangor, County Down, had been leading missions and revivals throughout Britain and Ireland since the turn of the twentieth century. He found, though, a particularly receptive audience for his United Gospel Campaign in Northern Ireland in the period immediately following Partition. John Long, a contemporary of Nicholson's and a founder member of the Go-Preachers, makes a direct connection between the religious fervour that swept the North in those years and the vicious sectarian violence that preceded it:

> During the last three years, the city of Belfast suffered much
> from lawlessness, and political agitation and bigotry. During
> the tribulation of those days the saints met together in their
> homes and missions to pray for a revival, and protection, and
> peace, and their enemies. That was followed with a time of
> salvation, and refreshing all over the city.*

So successful was Nicholson that, legend has it, in the Belfast
shipyards, which in 1920 had seen the mass expulsion of
Catholics, a special shed had to be erected to house the stolen
tools returned by repentant workers. Legend does not say
whether similar measures were taken to facilitate the return
of their former Catholic colleagues. Maybe Nicholson only
dealt in the smaller kind of miracle.

Nicholson preached in Railway Street Presbyterian Church
in Lisburn on 25th October 1924. If that was the site of
Jack's life-change then he soon veered away from his mentor,
who continued all his life to preach from church pulpits.
(WP, noted John Long, seemed to have been 'specially raised
up for that purpose'.) Jack gravitated to the Plymouth
Brethren, for whom the pulpit was a symbol of hierarchy
and false division: they met in the round, all 'saints' alike. He
gravitated very particularly to the Exclusive Brethren, who

---

* *The Journal of John Long III*, Volume 7, January 1923 (see http://home.-
earthlink.net/~truth444/JohnLong/index-JohnLong.html). Long's journal is a
remarkable insight into the whole subculture of revivalist sects criss-crossing
these islands in the decades either side of 1900, although you could be
forgiven at times for thinking that really there was only one modest-sized sect
and an enormous number of pseudonyms. The Go-Preachers (from Jesus'
injunction to his disciples in Matthew 10:7, 'as ye go, preach') were also
known as Irvinites, Cooneyites, Two-by-twos, Black Stockings, Dippers, the
Damnation Army, the Truth, the Way, and even the Church with No Name.

had split from the Open Brethren in 1848, it being a quirk of
the Brethren that far from uniting believers as they had set
out to do they had themselves split into ever smaller,
mutually hostile groupings. The initial schism occurred less
than twenty years after the first appearance of the Plymouth
Brethren.

'Exclusive' in Brethren terms refers to the refusal to accept
into one 'fellowship' someone already excluded, for whatever
reason, from another. The Exclusives' name for such a person
is 'leper'.* It also refers to the members' desire to exclude
from their lives all the evils of the modern world, wherever
they might be lurking.

When his eldest son, David, won a prize in Lisburn's
Market Square school in the mid-1930s, Jack refused to
attend the ceremony. Market Square was a Presbyterian school.
Sending his children there was one thing – they had to go
somewhere after all – but to cross the threshold himself would
have compromised his Exclusive Brethren principles. Later, in
1949, he declined the invitation to David's wedding rather
than set foot in a church. David sat across the table from him
in the kitchen of 9 Antrim Street and tried to get

---

* For the leper's anguish see again *The Journal of John Long*, the third volume
this time, where he tells of his own expulsion from the Go-Preacher
fellowship over the question of whether clergymen were beyond redemption.
'Then Irvine tested the meeting and asked all those who believe that there
are clergymen born again? [sic] And there were only two stood up, namely
[Goodhand] Pattison and I. Then he asked all those who believe that there
never was or never could be a clergyman born again to stand up, and every
one of them stood up, except two, and there were fully 200 people present.
Then Irvine warned me not to visit any saint's house, but to go on fresh
ground for myself, and if I came back after twelve months believing that
clergyman were saved, they would look upon me as being unsaved too; that
cut the last thread of my fellowship with them, so I left in tears.'

him to change his mind. Surely for just one day – for an hour, a *wedding* – he could make an exception. Jack was unbending. 'It's my belief,' he said, and, when David pressed him to come along to the reception at least: 'I just can't.'

David did, in between times, score one small victory over the Brethren, badgering and badgering for a wireless set so that he could listen to Joe Louis defend his heavyweight title against Welshman Tommy Farr, the 'Tonypandy Terror', in New York's Yankee Stadium in August 1937. (I was going to say that the wireless to the Brethren was the internet of its day, then remembered the tens of thousands of Brethren-related sites I had come across in the course of my research.) Louis edged the title bout on points, but Farr, who fought all but the first few rounds with gashes above both eyes, was considered by many watching – and listening – to be the real winner. Actually, the outcome in Antrim Street too was less clear-cut than it had first appeared. Jack might have raised high the sash windows to allow neighbours gathered in the street to follow the action from the Yankee Stadium, but although the radio remained in the house for the best part of forty years after the Louis–Farr fight it was rarely on again, and almost never for anything other than the news.*

For most of that time Jack had attended a meeting hall above a shoe-mender's on Antrim Street itself, although 'hall' might give a misleading impression. When it came to ostentation the Exclusive Brethren took a double-yellow-line

---

* There is a clash of memories here. My father can faintly recall the wireless – it was a KB, or Kolster Brandes – being carried into the house by his Uncle David's son, yet another Phares, who worked in a wireless supplier's in Belfast. This Phares, however, was killed in a traffic accident in February 1935, two and a half years before Louis and Farr touched gloves, and two months before my father turned three.

approach: none at all at all. Jack and Kate, living practically on the doorstep, were unofficial caretakers. They would cross the street every Saturday night to prepare the hall for the next day's meeting, dusting the benches, sweeping and mopping the floor. My cousin Ella, who often helped out with the cleaning, also went to the Sunday meeting. She talks of 'hard hymns', sung without accompaniment, and usually with Jack in the lead. Ella sat at the back with Kate. (So not quite 'in the round' then.)

'She wasn't as deeply into it as he was,' says Ella, who herself went as much for something to do on a Sunday. It could be like that, Lisburn, even when I was living there at the turn of the nineties.

Kate had no trouble accepting the invitation to David's wedding. She waved goodbye to Jack that morning from the back of the taxi David had booked for her and carried on waving to the pedestrians she passed until she reached the church at Lambeg where her son was to marry Naomi Turkington.

I like to imagine she had a new hat for the occasion. Hats were her particular weakness: hats and jumble sales and more often than not the two together.

David told me he thought a lot of the fun had gone out of Kate's life after Jack's conversion. This was the night of the big archive-handover (and of that Manchester United victory at Highbury . . . did I say it was 4–2?). We were sitting by now in the dining room of my house, the papers he and Edmund and my father had brought with them spread all over the table: rent books, wartime identity cards, their cousin Phares's family tree, diaries, of course, wills, birth certificates, funeral receipts – a disproportionate number of funeral receipts. Mostly, though, we were talking. Mostly David was. He was the eldest of the three brothers; he had the most to say.

Kate had been fond of Irish dancing when she was younger, he told me. In fact, she had taught him. She played the mouth organ, too, and had a good untrained singing voice.* David would wake in the mornings to the sound of this voice rising through his floorboards from the scullery, would join in with it on occasion, lying there in bed: 'The Fairy Queen', 'After the Ball', 'I Dreamt I Dwelt in Marbled Halls'. This last Kate would sometimes ask Jack to play for her on the flute.

He had been well known for playing the flute in his earlier life when he was variously (on occasion simultaneously) bandmaster, secretary, and librarian of Lisburn Conservative Flute Band, several times the all-Ireland champions. In this earlier life too he had been a founder member of the Lisburn Choral Society, later Lisnagarvey Operatic. His 1960 diary has a newspaper clipping pasted on the front cover, with a picture of Giuseppe Verdi above the legend 'he quoted 150,000 francs – and got the Khedive's commission'. I am assuming it was put there by way of admiration, not admonition for implied greed. His own singing voice, a tenor, was more than decent, and even after his conversion he could turn it to secular tunes. One neighbour, 'Wee' Billy Bingham, a widower and veteran of the Great War, rolling home drunk from McKenny's Bar on the corner of Antrim Street and Bow Street, would regularly stumble in the door of number 9 and refuse to budge until Jack had sung 'If Those Lips Could Only Speak'.

* In later years she was fond of television as well, on the rare occasions she got to see it in one of her children's houses. 'She would have sat there and tittered,' my mother says. A great verb, titter; it is Kate to a triple-t.

He stood in a beautiful mansion
Surrounded by riches untold
As he gazed at a beautiful picture
That hung in a frame of gold
Was a picture of a lady
So beautiful young and fair
To this beautiful lifelike picture
He murmured in sad despair

If those lips could only speak, if those eyes could only see
If those beautiful golden tresses were here in reality
Could I only take your hand as I did when you took my name
But it's only a beautiful picture in a beautiful golden frame

I realise, transcribing these words, that the picture I see in my mind's eye, like the picture I never did see upstairs in Antrim Street, has a triangular frame.

Whatever it was Wee Billy Bingham saw in his mind's eye he would, as my father tells it, 'have a good cry and go home happy'. The small printing works he owned further down Antrim Street had penny song-sheets of Orange standards permanently on display in the front window. It was from these that my father, forehead pressed against the glass, hands cupped to keep the glare out of his eyes, learned the words of 'The Sash' and 'Derry Walls' ('up to our necks in Fenian blood' and all that), which would tend to suggest that this particular, Protestant form of popular song was not at all the sort of thing he was used to hearing at home.

Maybe there was an upside to the dearth of fun David mentioned that night in my dining room.

Kate when she died left no written record to corroborate or contradict his hunch. Actually she seems never to have learned to write much more than her name . . . whichever version of it she was using at any given moment. Jack left any amount of material, besides his Faith Mission diaries, but precious little of it from before his conversion. Of all his children only the eldest, Eileen, knew the Jack who felt he needed saving when W. P. Nicholson blew in and out of town. Which brings me to the last of the problems with dates – and names.

Eileen was born on 30th September 1915 – a Thursday according to the day-finding chart – ten and a half years before David, who was followed in fairly short order by Jackie (christened John Edmund), my father, and Edmund, who leapfrogged a 'William' to land on his second, given name.

Eileen in the family is a version of Eleanor. There is in the same generation a cousin Eileen, born only a couple of years after my aunt, and baptised as Eleanor after their common grandmother. My own cousin Ella's name is, of course, a more usual short form of the same name. It would seem reasonable to assume that my aunt started life as an Eleanor too. It is certainly what her brothers had always assumed, although admittedly her birth certificate was not among the papers they brought with them to my house. She was so much older than them, none of them thought it unusual that they had never seen it.

In fact, her name is entered in the official register as Eileen, plain and simple. It is not entered at all, however, until January 1928, when she is already twelve years old, when Eleanor, her not-quite namesake, is exactly three years dead.*

Then again it seems a lot of things had to be put on hold until Eleanor had died. Like Jack and Kate appearing on the same electoral register; like their wedding, which took place on the morning of Friday 6th February 1925, in Lisburn's Christ Church, less than three weeks after Eleanor's funeral.

'First came love, then the carriage, and ten years later came the marriage.'

No wonder they didn't go in for anniversaries.

He was thirty-one, she thirty. The marriage certificate gives their ages as thirty and twenty-five respectively. It gives

* A letter to Jack from the General Registrar Office in London, dated 24th October 1927, re-directing his enquiry – about an earlier, lost certificate? – to the Registrar General in Dublin, suggests that Jack had been struggling for some time with the post-Partition verification of this pre-Partition event.

my grandmother's name as Kathleen. It does not explain (OK, so I am being rhetorical here, it was never going to explain) why a man who may already have been carrying inside him the seed of Exclusive-Brethren re-birth should have chosen a Church of Ireland church for his wedding (some Exclusives you feel would as soon he had jumped the broom as walked the aisle), or for that matter why his bride should not have wanted the ceremony to be conducted in her own church, which was St Patrick's on Chapel Hill; which was Catholic. As far as I can tell she never again returned to her church, unless it was for family funerals, but sat and kept her own counsel at the back of the hall above the shoe-mender's that she had helped to clean the night before. Not that the Brethren could give a stuff* about what church you had left to join their fellowship. Indeed given how easily in the end my grandparents 'fixed' the problem of different faiths it might seem surprising that they did not get around to it sooner, but that is to make the mistake of assuming that everyone concerned cared to have it fixed at all, or at least of assuming that Eleanor did.

* I am assured that the term surfaces once in the Apocrypha.

Corner Shop

Eleanor Spence's own wedding, forty-seven years to the day before she died, took place not in Cargycreevy nor any of the neighbouring townlands, but in the same Railway Street Presbyterian Church where W. P. Nicholson would later preach. (The church had only been opened in 1864 to cope with the conversions from an earlier revival.) It seems that either she or Phares might already have been living in Lisburn, or even – Heaven forfend! – that the two of them might have been living there together. Early in the new year of 1878 the couple became the leaseholders of a grocer's shop at 22 Smithfield in the town's centre.

Lisburn is a city nowadays, albeit at time of writing the only city in Europe without a hotel.* The core of it, though, remains little changed from the earliest maps, which resemble nothing so much as the diagram of the female reproductive system, as laid out on page forty-three of my first-year

---

* At time of writing, on the other hand, there is a proposal for several hotels, a national sports stadium and – because, as football fans here sing, we're not Brazil, we're Northern Ireland – a conflict-resolution centre, to be built on the site of the former Maze prison, aka Long Kesh, within the borough boundary.

biology textbook, turned on its side. (Sideways, as I recall it, seemed as plausible a way as any to view that diagram in first year.) Two roads, roughly corresponding to the fallopian tubes, lead into the uterus that is Market Square. Or not-quite-square. The road on the left, working back from the 'square', is first Castle Street and then Seymour Street and then the Belfast Road. On the right, and still working back, Bridge Street takes you down a steep hill (although the declivity is lost on the map), across the River Lagan, out of County Antrim and into County Down. Sloan Street, a continuation of Bridge Street, soon becomes the Saintfield Road, veering to the south-east. Lisnastrain, where Eleanor was living before she met Phares, lies two miles further on.

But I am up around the liver now: back to the diagram.

Where Market Square starts to taper at the other end (actually, maybe leave the gynaecological analogy aside altogether), Bow Street begins, turning as it passes the mouth of Antrim Street and rising – again invisibly on the map – on to Chapel Hill and Longstone Street beyond.*

The true picture is, of course, a lot more complex than the outline described. (As was page forty-three of the biology textbook: the lesson of the summer after third year.) There are several other significant streets, many, many more entries and lanes. One of these, Haslem's Lane – or Haslam's, or Haslim's, or even Hazel – is reached through an archway, two-thirds of the way down Bow Street, on the left as you come from Market Square. Smithfield – squarer than Market Square – is at the bottom of the lane. Number 22 is the building on the corner.

* Just to confuse matters Market Square was originally Market Place, which name was subsequently transplanted to this junction of Bow Street and Chapel Hill.

In 1878 Smithfield was the site of the Tuesday pork market. There was also a cattle market, opening off the west side of Haslem's Lane, as well as a hay market and a potato, oats and grain market. It was not the worst place to be opening a shop, however unprepossessing.

And 22 Smithfield was pretty unprepossessing. The valuation list for 1878 (occupier Mr *Ferris* Patterson) describes it simply as a house and yard. Its rent of £2 0s 0d is in the lowest band for the area.

Lisburn at that time had a population of just over ten thousand and could trace its origins as a town back to the early decades of the seventeenth century when land seized, or inveigled, from the hapless Con O'Neill of Claneboye (family crest the Red Hand) was 'settled' by Sir Fulke Conway,* whose family seat was at Ragley Hall in Warwickshire. He chose as his

---

* The history that follows (it runs to eight pages, so you can skip it if you want to, although I warn you, you will miss a skite across to Paris) draws heavily on *Lisburn: the Town and its People, 1871–1973*, by Brian Mackey (Blackstaff Press, 2000) and on Fred Kee's *Lisburn Miscellany*, published by the Lisburn Historical Society in 1976.

stronghold a hill overlooking the Lagan, known as *Lios na gCearbhach*, or Lisnagarvey. In the Irish it means the 'fort of the gamesters', a reference, it seems, to the site's reputation as a gambling den in the days before Conway and his kind came calling. By the middle of the 1620s Sir Fulke's E-shaped mansion was surrounded by gardens with an orchard running down the slope towards the river, although Sir Fulke himself had not lived long to enjoy it. On his death in 1624 he was succeeded by his brother, Sir Edward. ('Sir' obviously ran in their family the way Phares did in ours.) A church had been established and substantial houses built on the streets either side – the modern Castle Street and Bridge Street – leading to a market house and square. The population had risen to about two hundred and fifty when, in 1641, much of the town was burned to the ground in a pivotal battle during the rising of the native Irish against the settlers: a battle that, paradoxically, the settlers won, in all probability saving Belfast in the process. For its first-degree pains Charles II, on his accession, awarded Lisnagarvey a Royal Charter, elevating its church to a cathedral and kick-starting the growth that helped the reconstructed town become in little more than half a century the eighth largest in Ireland.

In 1707 the town burned again, rather less gloriously, in a blaze started by turf ashes thrown on a dung heap by a Widow Walsh of Sluice Street.* How long the dung heap

---

* The widow's name comes not from Mackey, or Kee, but from a tract produced by the Plantation Gospel Hall to mark the tercentenary of her carelessness and pushed through my brother Paul's letterbox one early summer evening. The tract points out that the fire of 1707 was neither the first nor the last in the town, mentioning the years 1641 and 1920, before concluding cryptically, 'and they always happened on a Sunday . . . but that's another story'. Actually the third fire is in large part this story, but believe me, Sunday or no Sunday, there is nothing supernatural about its causes.

had been standing exactly is not recorded, although a bylaw of 1689 had forbidden any dung heap to remain for longer than three days in the open street before the door, which last two phrases would seem to me to leave a little too much wriggle room. (Do you know, I am almost sorry I wrote that.) But still, there was a heap, there was a widow; there were ashes. It being a Sunday, it being the early eighteenth century, it being Lisburn, most of the townsfolk were in church, which, while it prevented loss of life, meant that by the time the alarm was raised the flames had taken a firm grip. By four o'clock when the fire was finally brought under control there were scarcely two walls in the town left standing together. Not even the cathedral was spared. The congregation watched from behind the tombstones as the flames crept closer and closer then with a roar devoured it.

(You'll allow me the roar, I hope.)

My father always told me that this second fire was the reason for Lisnagarvey, the Irish gambler's paradise, becoming no-nonsense Lis*burn*. It sounds too hokey to be true, but in fact the only other commonly advanced explanation for the name is the proximity of the Lagan 'burn'. There is, though, nothing 'small' or 'brook-like' about the Lagan as it passes through Lisburn – it is wide enough for there to be an island just below the old castle; the island wide enough to have held a mill, now the civic centre – and besides, Lisburn was noted in the seventeenth and eighteenth centuries for its English, rather than Scottish, character.

The Lisnagarvey name lingers still here and there – in the town's hockey club, for instance, in the Operatic Society, in the high school my brother Paul attended; but whether in fact or in popular myth the flames coming up from Sluice Street had purged the town of its previous, rakish associations.*

A plaque in the market house commemorating its second rebuilding gives an indication of the chastened mood abroad in the town in the wake of the fire:

1708

> The year above this house erected
> This town was burnt ye year before
> People therein may be directed
> God hath judgments still in store
> And that they do not him provoke
> To give to them a second stroke
> The builder also doth desire ~
> At expiration of his lease ~
> The landlord living at that time
> May think upon the builders case.

This market house's remains in turn now form part of the Irish Linen Centre and Lisburn Museum in whose top-floor reading room, with its view down Bow Street towards the archway into Haslem's Lane, Antrim Street just beyond, I have researched much of the history I am relating. (The plaque itself has been relocated to the museum's lobby, right

---

* Curiously Henry Bayly, one of the town's earliest historians, attributes the name change to the earlier, 1641, conflagration. Some more recent historians, on the other hand, suggest that the names Lisnagarvey and Lisburn had always co-existed, referring to neighbouring Irish forts. The latter simply won out by dint of being easier for the English to get their tongues around. Having grown up listening to London newsreaders mangle every place name with more syllables than Doagh – hang on, including Doagh (it's *Doke*, you Doaghps) – I could easily be persuaded of this.

above the service doors into the coffee shop. Stand too long peering up at it and you are liable to get a trolley in the shins.) It was linen that made, or rather remade, Lisburn. The trade was already flourishing before the 1707 fire, thanks in no small part to the efforts of Louis Crommelin, a French Huguenot refugee, who established a colony of Huguenots – a colony, more to the point, of master weavers – in Lisnagarvey during the reign of William III. By the end of the eighteenth century the town was experiencing the same economic boom as Belfast and much of the rest of northeast Ulster. Experiencing too the upsurge in radical politics that so characterised Belfast in particular. When next there was a rising in Ireland, in 1798, it was in the name of Catholic, Protestant, and Dissenter.

The leader of this 'Society of United Irishmen' in Lisburn was Henry Munro, a merchant of Market Square, or as one contemporary report would have it, 'a little hot-headed fellow, who kept a shop . . . and bought Brown Linen'. In fairness to Munro, later accounts are rather more flattering:

In person he was remarkably handsome, he was exceedingly fond of dressing with neatness and taste. A portion of his black hair, in keeping with the fashion of the times, was worn very long and tied with a black ribbon hung over the collar of his coat. His conduct in his private life has been described as that of a perfect gentleman. He was fond of fun – a rather dashing personality. These were his characteristics. Some instances of his bravery have been related. When attending a linen market in Lurgan, a fire broke out [sic] in a local church. Munro personally, at great risk to himself, was mainly responsible for the quenching of the flames.

Of course he was. He was a Lisburn man. Fire was practically mother's milk to him.*

Like many of his fellow United Irishmen, Munro had formerly been a member of the Volunteer Movement, which had grown up in the late 1770s to repel any opportunistic attempts at invasion while the regular army was tied up in its war with the rebel American colonies. The French, as ever, were the greatest concern, although a tablet in Lisburn Cathedral commemorates Lieutenant William Dobbs, killed in an engagement with the American privateer Paul Jones who ventured up Belfast Lough in 1778. Six years earlier Benjamin Franklin had come to meet Lord Hillsborough, Secretary of State for the Colonies, at his castle just south of Lisburn to try to defuse the growing tension. The meeting was a failure, to the extent that Hillsborough was later dubbed the birthplace of the American Revolution. Franklin himself, however, like many another American statesman who has visited Hillsborough Castle since, made a big impression on those following events from the outside.† There was even a Dr Franklin Tavern, otherwise known as Peggy Barclay's, in Sugarhouse Entry off the High Street in Belfast. It was here, in the guise of the Muddlers' Club, that

* The little hot-headed Munro can be found in a history of Ballynahinch on Ros Davies's County Down website, the dashing personality in the journal of the Lisburn Historical Society, Volume 1, 1978.
† Since 1972 Hillsborough has been the official residence of the Secretary of State for Northern Ireland. During Peter Mandelson's tenure Ali, then managing a children's theatre company, was invited to a reception in the course of which Mandelson's dogs came scampering into the room. The Secretary of State called them to heel: 'Jack! Bobby!' 'Jack and Bobby as in Charlton?' asked Ali, who had come of age during the glory years of *Italia '90*. '*Kennedy*,' said Mandelson icily. 'I mean icily even for him,' Ali told me later, not the least put out. 'You could have sunk a liner with that look.'

the radicalised Volunteers who made up the United Irishmen first met. When revolution erupted in France, Belfast was in the vanguard of European cities sending congratulations.

It is easy to get carried away by all this, though, as easy as it was to get carried away by it back then. Ulster was at once the most radical part of the island and the most bitterly divided along sectarian lines. So, after leading his United Irishmen in a disastrous engagement with Crown forces and locally recruited yeomen at Ballynahinch in June of 1798, Munro – a better linen-trader alas than a general – was captured in the townland of Clintagooland, or Clintagullion (either way the name is priceless; 'meadow of the holly tree', it means) and brought back to Market Square to be hanged. His head – I am trying to keep the word 'hot' out of mine – and the heads of three other rebels were stuck on pikes at the four corners of the square, two of which I can see without leaving my chair in the Linen Centre's reading room, and Lisburn went back to being the safe Tory seat of its landlords, Sir Fulke Conway's descendants, the Hertford family.*

For much of the nineteenth century the Hertfords were conspicuous by their absence, the third and fourth marquises between them managing only six weeks in the town in more than fifty years. The third marquis – 'a wastrel who would do

* My father's cousin Phares mentions in a letter that one of the Cargycreevy Pattersons was a rebel pikeman at Ballynahinch. Certainly Munro mustered his forces – as well as he was able – at nearby Creevy Rocks, and there is a Patterson among the names of fifty wanted men published in the official 'Black List'. Let us hope he had better fortune in defeat than his commander, who paid a farmer called Billy Holmes five pounds and a linen shirt to hide him. Holmes pocketed the money, put on the shirt, covered Munro with weeds, and went and got the yeomen.

anything to acquire money' – was said to have been the model for the Marquis of Steyne in *Vanity Fair*. He was a pal of the Prince of Wales, later Prince Regent, later King George IV, who had a long affair with the marquis's own mother, Isabella Seymour Conway.* The fourth marquis preferred Paris to London and Lisburn (I know, can you believe it?) and built up what was soon a world-renowned art collection. When he died in 1870 without a legitimate heir the collection, the house in Paris and the town of Lisburn passed to his illegitimate son, Sir Richard Wallace. (The Marquis of Hertford title and other parts of the Lisburn estate went to a cousin.) Aged then in his early fifties, Sir Richard had for many years been his father's agent at auctions and at the time of his accession had just come through the Franco-Prussian War, during which he had gained a reputation as a major philanthropist. Mindful of the hardships endured by his fellow Parisians during the Prussian siege and the Commune that followed, Sir Richard gifted the French capital fifty cast-iron drinking fountains – still referred to there as 'Les Wallaces' – and had five of an identical 'French Renaissance' design installed in Lisburn, which he visited for the first time on Valentine's Day 1873. It was a whirlwind romance. Thousands turned out to greet his carriage, which was pulled for the final half mile to the town centre by a team of over-exuberant young men (they still exist, although these days they prefer to leave you on the kerbside before they run off with the vehicle), and Wallace, although not actually moved to live in the town, was enamoured enough to return at regular intervals and to foot the bill for a programme of

* See 'Prinny's Set' at www.georgianindex.net. Isabella's cuckolded husband, marquis number two, was another early member of the set.

long-overdue improvements, including a Palladian court-house and yet another makeover for the market house.

Two years after his death, in 1890, a memorial – 'rather disappointing, stone Gothic' – was erected in Castle Gardens, opposite his official residence, to go with the fountains, the high school he had endowed, and a twenty-five-acre park, on the northern outskirts of town, bearing his name.*

Phares and Eleanor by the turn of that decade had five children: William Edmund, David (the names echo down through the generations), Agnes, Emma Harriet, and 'Fred'. A sixth child, 'the first Emma' (in fact the first Emma Harriet) had died in 1886 before her second birthday. Phares in particular took the death hard. Ninety years later his youngest son, Jack, then embarking, if he had but known it, on his own last year, transcribed these lines into his 1975 diary:

> We had a child, a fair sweet child
> Her age we cannot tell
> They reckon not by years and months
> Where she has gone to dwell.
>
> To us for eighteen anxious months
> Her infant smiles were given
> Then she bade farewell to earth
> And went to live in heaven.

---

* The school, originally the Lisburn Intermediate and University School, became Wallace High in 1942. The verdict on the memorial is Charles Brett's (soon to be met in larger font and unencumbered by asterisks) from the snappily titled *List of Historic Buildings, Groups of Buildings, Buildings of Architectural Importance in the Borough of Lisburn*, first published by the Ulster Architectural Heritage Society in 1969. Long out of print, but saved for the world at www.lisburn.com.

And below: 'One of the many verses written by my father in remembrance of Emma who died in infancy.'

Phares had the full poem (there are another eight lines) printed up by the *Lisburn Herald* and hung in a mahogany frame in the living quarters in Smithfield, which I can only imagine made for curious, not to say uncomfortable, reading for the second Emma.

When Jack was born in early 1893 Phares and Eleanor were prospering. A combination of good location and strong family connections made them the first port of call for many farmers coming in to Lisburn market from the rich County Down hinterland. They were happy to accept payment in kind, knowing that any produce they came by that way would be sold on again at a profit. The corner shop had expanded into number 39 Haslem's Lane, adjoining 22 Smithfield. By the time of the next census, in 1901, it had expanded again, taking in 37 Haslem's Lane as well, and had been re-designated a first-class house, the only one in the immediate vicinity, with nine rooms in occupation by the family and – the real arbiter of class, it seems – ten windows facing on to the street.

A photograph taken towards the end of 1893 shows seven of those ten windows. Two, either side of the shop door, bear adverts for tea and Cadbury's Cocoa. Sacks of meal are visible through the panes on the left, canned goods on the right in front of what might be a portrait of Queen Victoria (the edges of the photograph are somewhat faded), or, less patriotically, a Pears Soap woman.

In the doorway itself Eleanor stands, the most clearly visible of a group that includes a 'Nurse Rainey', whose married name was actually Hopkins, and two young Hopkins children; includes too, although he is only a white smear

against the dark of the shop's interior, Jack, in the arms of a sibling (judging by the height) whose face has also faded with time.

Eleanor is, to go by the adjustment to her death certificate, forty-one, but you can see how she could get away with a decade less. Her dark hair is parted in the centre and pulled back behind her ears, and she wears a scarf – it has the look of silk – knotted casually at her throat. Her mouth is open in a half smile and there is an openness too, a freshness, in her expression, so that it is hard to get your head around the fact that her life began before official records were kept. She looks, amid the bleached and blurred faces, the sacks of meal and nameless tea ads, next to the nurse's starched white collar and cape, out of her time. You do not have to be family to recognise her. A change of clothes (but don't lose the silk scarf), a few days' acclimatisation, and you get the feeling she would fit right into our world, even though the shop door she is standing in is now protected by metal shutters, rarely lifted, and has a sign above it saying Lisburn Homing Pigeon Club, and even though the Smithfield end of Haslem's Lane has lately become the gateway to a new shopping mall, Lisburn Square (think Wetherspoon's, think Argos, think wherever you live), replacing the swimming pool, which thirty-five years ago replaced the egg-grading factory, which in turn replaced the potato, oats and grain market that Eleanor would have seen if she happened to glance to the right of the camera that day in 1893.

She was, after all, a developer herself. Around the time the photograph was taken she and Phares, or (variation number 142) *Faris* this time on the deeds, bought a row of eight properties under construction on Templemore Street in east Belfast. This was at the height of Victorian Belfast's economic expansion, when the city's housing stock quadrupled in thirty years and the population increased by a third in a mere ten.* Templemore Street, off the Albertbridge Road, half a mile over the River Lagan from the city centre, was within walking distance of Harland and Wolff, the world's biggest shipyard (but you knew that), of the world's biggest ropeworks (possibly even that) and of the world's leading manufacturer of ventilation fans, the Sirocco Works. (Have your family always lived here?) If you had a bit of money to invest the opportunities existed in Belfast to make a whole lot more. Actually, if you have a bit of money to invest right this

---

* Jonathan Bardon, *Belfast: An Illustrated History* (Blackstaff Press, 1982), p. 137. It is a fact insufficiently acknowledged that a great deal of the Belfast literature of the 1980s might never have turned out as it did – have turned out, some of it, at all – had it not been for Bardon's book. *Fat Lad* for one would have been a whole lot thinner.

minute the opportunities exist again, in exactly the same part of town. The ropeworks is a shopping centre, the Sirocco Works a temporary car park with planning permission for offices, retail units and apartments, and Harland and Wolff, aka the Titanic Quarter, has a fair claim to be one of the world's largest building sites: there is a whole other city being built out there.

The Lisburn papers of Eleanor's time regularly carried front-page ads offering new property for sale in Belfast, the east of the city in particular.

£765 – Twenty-two houses and shop, situate off Mount Street, lying between Woodstock and My Lady's Roads; net profit rental, £102 8s 6d; subject to £875 at 4½%; would make a capital investment; will sell to pay 14%.

£485 – Eight houses immediately off Castlereagh Road; net profit rent, £60; a well-built lot.

£300 – Three houses, Jocelyn Avenue; profit rent, £31 10s; a neat block.

Though eight miles distant from Belfast along the main road south out of the city, Lisburn always seems to come upon you unexpectedly quickly when approached from the east. A mile and a half along the Ormeau Road from Belfast city centre you arrive at the start of the Saintfield Road. Two miles further out, just before Carryduff, you pick up signs for Drumbo, 'City of Lisburn', a mile away. Lisnastrain, where Eleanor grew up, is on the edge of Drumbo parish. Many of its other townlands have long since been thought of as part of Greater Belfast.

When in the late 1960s my Uncle Edmund accompanied his father to the Templemore Street houses, then in need of serious repair, the handyman who met them there was a Dunwoody.

It seems likely that even before the boom times began there were family ties to east Belfast, more than likely – although the deeds have not survived – that Phares and Eleanor's portfolio extended well beyond Templemore Street and terraced houses. Over the next few years, bars began to feature heavily in their story. There was a bar on Templemore Street itself, 'shop' apparently being an elastic term in the 1890s, another bar off the neighbouring Woodstock Road, and a third somewhere across the river: the Falls Road in the west and the Antrim and Crumlin Roads in the north have all been suggested, and are all possibilities since, perplexingly, you can arrive at Lisburn by carrying on up the Falls and on to the Glen Road, or by heading in what feels like the wrong direction entirely, over the hills at the top of the Crumlin. Which might explain why for years every train leaving Belfast, no matter what its destination, seemed obliged to halt for half an hour in Lisburn station.*

Wherever this third bar was, and however much family backing Phares and Eleanor had had when they first took on the corner shop, this was all still pretty impressive progress in little more than fifteen years. And it was not as if they had had to scrimp and save to get there. All the indications are

---

* A royal train carrying the Prince and Princess of Wales stopped there briefly in 1885 (Mackey, p. 39). Credit for the event went to Sir Richard Wallace, a personal friend (chumminess with Princes of Wales being another of his inheritances), although knowing Lisburn station the miracle would have been if the train had got through without stopping.

that they had money to spare and the characters to revel in it. Phares was a member of a clique of Lisburn businessmen who went across to England each year for the racing festivals at Aintree and Cheltenham. In between times he liked to keep his gambling-hand in at the Maze races, a short jaunt from Lisburn town centre, or even closer to home with a game of cards. Actually, in the true spirit of *Lios na gCearbhach*, two flies, a wall and another mildly interested party appear to be all he needed to generate a bet, even if he did not always intend it to be taken seriously, at any rate not when he lost.

Whisper it, my great-grandfather had the reputation of being a welsher.

He was a member of the Masonic Order, lodge number 811, which had its seat in Castle Street and which provided the Lisburn papers with regular and untaxing copy.

At the recent dinner given by Bro. R. C. Browne, Bro. Joseph
Hope read the following and it was warmly applauded:

Dear Bro. Browne,
We meet tonight on true Masonic ground,
Not by vain words your praises here to sound,
But just to give our heartfelt feelings vent,
By practical, though slight, acknowledgment,
For what you've done these years, I think nigh-seven,
For Masonry and Number Eight-Eleven.
With heart and hand congratulations we
Now offer you on reaching that degree
Called matrimonial bliss – and, on the square,
I'm sure the ladies wish more Masons there,

And willingly would lend a hand, always,
To that degree to bachelor Masons raise,
And tie that knot firm as Masonic grip,
Which ne'er till death we hope will prove a slip.

The Great Grand Master ever deign to bless
Your lives with love, health, wealth and happiness . . .

And so it goes on, for line after perfectly rhyming line, until the final rousing couplet:

May we all meet in that Grand Lodge in Heaven,
Is Hope's heart's wish for you and Eight-Eleven.

Brother Hope had the ideal job for musing on his end rhymes, he kept a hackney cab and frequently drove brethren to meetings and socials in Masonic halls the length and breadth of Antrim and Down.

Immediately below this particular *jeu d'esprit* in the *Lisburn Standard* of 10th February 1894 – and in apparently unintentional counterpoint – is an ad, which runs, with a circumlocution typical of the period,

Love, courtship and marriage are naturally subjects of interest for every young girl. The chief ambition is to have a rich husband and an extensive establishment, but her ideas become greatly modified as her experience of the world grows more matured. At last she settles down to the conviction that riches do not mean happiness, and she determines to be content with true worth, even if allied to comparative poverty. When she comes to this frame of mind she makes herself worthy to be a true helpmate to the man of her choice. Her first duty is to obtain the blessing of sound health; Holloway's pills will give all that is required in this direction if taken regularly.

How greatly Eleanor's ideas had become modified in the sixteen years of her marriage to Phares might be measured by her decision always to keep a barrel of porter on the go above the shop to entice her husband to spend more time at Number Twenty-Two than at Number Eight-Eleven. Not that she was averse to drink in the house for drink's sake: gin, not Holloway's, was her preferred helpmate's little helper. And she had her own set of friends with whom she regularly socialised: again the name Dunwoody crops up.

As for matters of wealth, two legal documents from this period afford a glimpse into the couple's financial affairs. The first, dated 6th March 1891, is the last will and testament of Jane Shallow, spinster of Smithfield, who died five weeks later on 12th April, leaving all her worldly goods, amounting to £264 – or four times the annual profit on eight houses off the Castlereagh Road – to Eleanor.* The second is a bill that Phares received from Charley & Allen solicitors in the spring of 1893. Throughout the winter just ended he had had been pursuing a debt of £130 from a man called Carlin. The solicitors' itemised costs tell the story of the pursuit. At Phares's request, on 29th November, a writ is drawn up and

* All her worldly goods, that is, apart from her writing desk and dressing case, which were left to Eleanor's son David, then aged twelve (I am sure the dressing case came in handy), and a legacy of one shilling to Jane Shallow's cousin Mrs Lizzie Barden, who lived in Dublin at 68 Eccles Street, five doors down from what is now Bloom House. One whole shilling. Knock yourself out, Lizzie.

> BE IT KNOWN, that on the 4th day of May 189), the last Will and Testament , hereunto annexed, of
>
> _Jane Mary Ann Shallow (in Will called "Jane Shallow") late of Smithfield Lisburn, in the county of Antrin Ulster_
>
> deceased, who died on or about the 12th day of April 1891, at _Dame Place_
>
> and who at the time of _her_ death had a fixed place of abode at _Dame Place_ within the District of _Belfast_
>
> was proved, and registered in the District Registry of the said Division at _Belfast_ and that the administration of all and singular the personal estate and effects of the said deceased was granted by the aforesaid Court to
>
> _Eleanor Patterson of Smithfield, Lisburn aforesaid (Wife of Phares Patterson) the Sole Executrix_

delivered to the Belfast company of Alexander & Irvine for service (two pounds ten shillings). Four days later Phares asks that the writ be recalled (three-and-five) as he 'expected to get the defendant in Belfast on Wednesday'. On Thursday he writes to say that Carlin was not in Belfast after all, but that he has heard he will definitely be at the Enniskillen Fair on Monday. Charley & Allen dispatch the writ (three-and-five again) to a certain Flood in Enniskillen for service there. Carlin, however, does not appear, on the Monday of the fair or the Tuesday.

Carlin is finally run to ground, the writ served, in Belfast on Christmas Eve. (No charge for that, but ten shillings and sixpence in sundries.) Less than a week later, on 30th December, Phares instructs Charley & Allen not to proceed further at present. The solicitors are understandably perplexed. They write three shillings and five pence-worth of letter asking that Phares let them know whether he has seen or heard from Carlin as, if not, it will be necessary that the affidavit be sent for swearing. In January another letter is dispatched (you can guess how much by now) asking what arrangement Phares has made regarding the writ. Two days later his reply arrives, informing the solicitors that he has hopes of seeing Carlin after the Belfast Fair . . .

There is more than a whiff in all of this of secret deals and handshakes, of the law as a last resort, which even then can be circumvented. The final act of the cost-column drama, therefore, makes interesting reading despite its air of anti-climax. On 18th January Phares accepts a cheque for thirty-nine pounds, or something under a third of the sum origin-ally sued for, from a man named McAleer who has (I am guessing not out of the goodness of his heart) taken on Carlin's debt. It is difficult to know whether Phares would have looked on this as ninety-one pounds lost, or thirty-nine gained, whether the original debt related to goods and services not paid for, or to yet another bet (the welsher welshed?); but at least by paying Charley & Allen in cash he saved himself nineteen shillings from his bill of six pounds, twelve shillings and a penny. I have no doubt he spent his windfall wisely.

In the autumn of the following year, 1894, Phares went with three other members of his Eight-Eleven Lodge to Cargycreevy Masonic Hall on the Old Ballynahinch Road, close to where he was born and a hundred yards or so from the Presbyterian church with the tombstones of two of his namesakes. (The hall and the church, in fact, constitute the nearest thing that Cargycreevy has to a centre.) These family ties, not to mention Phares's convenient location next to Smithfield market, might have accounted for the close relationship between the lodge here and his own in Castle Street. You can still see his signature in the guest book from a previous visit on 14th October 1891, alongside his father William's and another of the district's legion Phares Pattersons.

This particular night the weather was cold and very wet. The hackney cab that delivered the Eight-Eleven men to the hall – in all probability Joseph Hope's – was late coming back for them. (Driver distracted perhaps by a trickier than expected couplet.) Rather than wait any longer, or stay the night with one or other of the Cargycreevy Pattersons, Phares, emboldened by the evening's drinking, decided to walk the four miles back to Lisburn. The road is long and straight, the country on either side open farmland most of the way. At that time of the year especially it can have afforded him scant protection from the rain. He arrived at Smithfield in the wee small hours soaked through, exhausted and, despite the walk he had had, despite the dousing, still not entirely sober. He did not make it as far as his bedroom, but fell asleep in a sitting-room armchair in his saturated woollen overcoat. Even nowadays this is not a good idea. In the late nineteenth century it was practically an invitation to pneumonia, which on this occasion did not need asking twice. Although he appeared to rally for a time, he never fully recovered from that night, and on 10th December 1894, at the age of thirty-eight, Brother Phares Patterson was finally called up to where the Great Grand Master sits. On 13th December his physical remains were conveyed in best oak coffin and four-in-hand hearse to the newly purchased family plot in Lisburn Cemetery's prominent 'Merchants' Row'. Two dozen mourning bands had been ordered up from the undertaker, James Abbott of Market Square. Seven were returned to him unused. A lot of mourners would have had their own bands then. Probably.

Phares had spent the last days of his illness in James Street, just across Haslem's Lane from the shop with his name on it. With him at the end, it says on his death certificate, was Charlotte Patterson, whoever she is. My father and his brothers do not remember ever hearing of a Charlotte, and such records as existed, and came through the Civil War unscathed, throw nothing up. Nor can anyone think of a reason why Eleanor was not there instead. Perhaps she had simply needed a break from his bedside. Or perhaps getting across the street to his bedside would have been the break. She had six children aged from sixteen down to twenty-two months (Jack). She had a shop to run. She had houses to manage, bars . . .

She had, although she did not know it yet, more bad news coming.

Widow

The week after Phares's funeral a ferocious storm hit Lisburn: the worst, according to those who could still remember that far back, since the legendary Big Wind of 1839.* In one of the most spectacular incidents the wind ripped a hundred and twenty feet of chimney off the Barbour Mill at Hilden and dumped it on nearby waste ground. It uprooted trees in Castle Gardens, sending one of them crashing through the roof and gable wall of the adjoining Sacred Heart of Mary Convent. Fortunately the dormitories were at the opposite end of the building. It carried away the thatched roofs from cottages at the bottom of Seymour Street, and further up the town, in Market Square, it destroyed the Salvation Army hall, leaving chairs driven into the ground by falling masonry. Number 22 Smithfield emerged with its roof and walls and windows intact, but Eleanor, with hindsight, could have been forgiven for seeing the

---

* I am reminded, writing 'Big Wind', of something the Belfast playwright Owen McCafferty once said about the beautiful literalness of English as it is spoken in the north of Ireland. We don't go to the cinema, we go to the 'pictures'. A kick in the arse is more precisely a boot up the hole, and twice as painful for its precision.

storms as a portent of the turbulent times that followed. (Tell me now, won't you, if you think I am overselling this . . .)

The family story goes like this. Some time in the year before Phares died he and Eleanor became owners of a property on the Dublin Road, or the Hillsborough Road as it is now more often referred to, about a mile from Lisburn town centre. Avonmore Lodge, my father told me the house was called, adding that 'Maginess the solicitor' lived there in later years, when my father was a boy.

In fact Brian Maginess, who inherited both Avonmore and his legal practice from his father, William George Maginess, was a barrister rather than a solicitor. Not only that, from 1938 to 1964 he was returned as a Unionist MP in the Northern Ireland Parliament, where he was at various times Minister of Public Security, Minister of Agriculture, Minister of Labour, Minister of Commerce, Minister of Home Affairs, Minister of Finance, and from 1945 a member of the Irish Privy Council. In 1956 he contributed a foreword to a government pamphlet, 'Why the Border Must Be', which concluded with what has to be one of the most flattering pictures ever painted of the Northern Irish state:

In World War II Ulster was a bridgehead between Europe and the United States. In this present [Cold] war of ideas we are still the bridgehead between a free Europe and a free America. We will hold the bridgehead so that one day the freedom which is here in Northern Ireland, in Great Britain and in the United States will lighten the whole world and mankind will enter into its rightful inheritance.*

* Quoted in the University of Ulster's Conflict Archive on the Internet, or CAIN. (You can imagine how pleased they were with that bit of Procrustean acronym-making. I suppose it beats CAROTIN.)

So *that's* what they were doing all those years when it looked to everyone else as though they were rigging electoral boundaries and discriminating against Catholics . . . But I am skipping forward a century.

Built in 1853, Avonmore Lodge sat on a rise in nine acres of land leased, like pretty much all of Lisburn at that time, from the fourth Marquis of Hertford: 'a handsome and commodious Residence, beautifully situated, with well-wooded Lawn and gate Lodge in front, and large garden at rere'. The house contained three reception rooms, five bedrooms, a WC (as modern as it got in 1853), servants' apartments, a whole complex of kitchens, pantries, dairies and china closets, as well as extensive office-houses, including stables for five horses, a coach-house, a harness-room, cart-sheds, byres, barns, piggeries, hen-runs and potato stores.

I think it is safe to say it had more than ten windows facing on to the street. I beg your pardon, the *grounds*.

The first owners were the Garrett family, who like the Maginesses after them had connections to the law as well as to the linen trade and the military. On 3rd August 1864 Robert Garrett, a sixty-three-year-old bachelor and colonel in the Indian Army, died at Avonmore. The death was registered by Henry John Garrett, brother of the deceased, who gave his address as Warren Cottage. This cottage, on an eight-acre site below Avonmore, was a significant house in its own right. Writing a hundred years later, Charles Brett (subsequently Sir Charles, future chair of the Ulster Architectural Heritage Society and the Northern Ireland Housing Executive and vice-chair of the Arts Council of Northern Ireland when I became a member in the mid-1990s, seven years after being sent to Lisburn as writer-in-the-community) describes Warren Cottage as a 'Pleasant plastered and creeper-covered two-storey house and outbuildings, overlooking Lagan Bridge and river, Regency glazing bars downstairs, Georgian upstairs'.*

It had long been home to a Miss Moore, famed far and wide for her charitable works – far enough and wide enough for the *Cavan Observer* to carry an obituary, singling out her contribution to the building of a church 'in one of the wildest districts of Connemara'. In Lisburn she lavished much time and energy on the home she established for 'unfortunate females'. Indeed according to the *Cavan Observer* it was the exertion and anxiety occasioned by the management of this home that brought on the fever that killed her. To this day many Lisburn people refer to the bridge here as Moore's Bridge, although from the time of her demise forward Warren Cottage and its inhabitants were very much satellites of the house at the top of the hill.

So, following his brother's death in 1864, Henry John Garrett graduated from the cottage to the larger lodge and when he died in 1893 he was succeeded by Benjamin Courtney Hobson, a Quaker, from Hillsborough, who had been residing in the cottage since 1889, the year after his marriage to Caroline Sinton, a fellow Quaker. Hobson's place in the cottage was taken by his brother-in-law Walter Sinton,

* From the short book with the long title already referred to. Sir Charles also wrote the essential *Buildings of Belfast 1700–1914*, first published in 1967, but best read in its revised 1985 edition, which catalogues the depredations of the intervening years' car bombings and bulldozings. One footnote, on the fate of the statue to the Revd Hugh Hanna in Carlisle Circus, reads, 'an early victim of the bombing, he was blown off his legs, and only his inscribed plinth remains, looking rather foolish'; another, simply, 'The goose died, and the Old Ministry of Commerce was knocked down, in the winter of 1966/7.'

who himself lived in the lodge for a time when Hobson eventually died.

It is important that I establish this line of succession, and highlight too the Quaker thread, because the family story goes on that having somehow come by Avonmore Lodge in that final year of his life, Phares then lost it in a side bet made at the Aintree Festival in April 1894. For reasons that no one now living can explain, however, the bet was not called in until after Phares's funeral that December, although no one living then could explain it to Eleanor's satisfaction either. She was beside herself with rage, fighting the claim in the courts and, when at last she was forced to concede defeat, insisting on a public handover of the deeds on the steps of Lisburn town hall. Even then she was not going to sully herself by being there in person. Instead she instructed her lawyers that the handover, in the presence of the town clerk, was to be performed by a 'Papish'. It was the greatest insult she could think of.*

'It's a great story, all right,' said the lawyer friend on whom I tested it, 'but I don't think there is a word of truth in it.'

The town-hall-steps tableau for a start was unlikely. Court rulings tended not to allow for such theatrical gestures, least of all on the part of the loser. And then, even though the firm of solicitors that acted for Eleanor might be gone (it was, I confirmed: long) and even though solicitors were in any case only obliged to hold on to files for twelve years, there would still be a paper trail.

---

* Not content with the greatest insult she added a curse for good measure: 'You will none of you die in your beds,' she warned. And – spooky, spooky – three of those the curse was aimed at (perhaps she had the entire opposition legal team in her sights) did not, including one of Lisburn's first road-traffic casualties.

Had I managed to find *any* supporting documents?

Well, I said, my Uncle David claimed to remember having seen 'some papers' when he was younger, going so far as to specify legal costs of a thousand pounds – enough then, someone else had suggested to me, to buy a fifty-acre farm in many parts of Ulster. As to where these papers might be now, however, there unfortunately his memory failed him.

My friend's look said that perhaps the papers, like the story, had acquired legs.

On his advice I went, where any methodical researcher would have gone to begin with, to Dublin, to the Registry of Deeds, a healthy distance from the Four Courts, in which most of the other national records were stored, and in 1922 destroyed.

I travelled without much expectation of success. After all, I had already found in various reading rooms and record offices up north the names of Avonmore's successive own-ers, their denominations even. (Maybe I was guilty of taking Quakerism at face value – all that soul-searching in recent years about whether to accept Lottery funds – but somehow I could not see Benjamin Courtney Hobson standing next to my great-grandfather against the rails at Aintree, roaring his horse home.) And, sure enough, I unearthed nothing in the registry to contradict what I had known of the line of succession when I boarded the train that morning in Belfast. I did at least, though, find something to pique my interest, something that is over and above the beautiful registry building itself and the walk to it from Connolly Station by way of Eccles Street, of Bloom House, and the house belonging to the cousin of the very late Jane Shallow. (What *did* she ever do with that yearly shilling?*) It came in the form of a memorial of deed poll, dated 6th February 1893, by Thomas L'Estrange, solicitor, 'reciting that the said Henry John Garrett died on 28th Jan 1893 without having revoked or altered his will. And reciting that the said Thos L'Estrange had declined to prove the said will or in any wise to administer to the estate of the said Henry John Garrett or to act or interfere in the trusts of the said will'. In fact, he 'absolutely and wholly renounced and disclaimed the offices of trustee and executor of the said will'.

For maybe twelve hours I allowed myself to imagine that this betokened a contested will – I mean, two verbs *and* two adverbs in that last sentence: he wasn't mucking about – leaving open a window of possibility for Phares and his Aintree bet to clamber through.

Then I spoke to another lawyer friend. (I hadn't dismissed the first one, he just wasn't home when I rang. OK, so maybe I didn't press the buttons all that hard.) I wouldn't get too excited, this friend said. The deed poll could simply be lawyer-speak for something altogether more mundane, one solicitor passing on work to another for whatever reason.

Like?

'Oh, I don't know – illness, retirement . . .'

Thomas L'Estrange – I looked him up the minute I was off the phone – was seventy years old in 1893. Originally from Dublin, he had been practising as a solicitor in his adopted

---

* Leopold Bloom's budget for 16th June 1904 throws up several possibilities: four pork kidneys, say, or sheep's trotters if preferred; twelve Banbury cakes, twelve Fry's plain chocolate bars, or a like number of tram fares, or there again half a dozen packets of notepaper and envelopes to let her friends know how truly blessed she was.

city of Belfast since 1847; that is, since three years before his marriage to one Sarah Garrett, sister of Robert and Henry . . .

'What was that banging?' Ali called to me from the foot of the stairs.

'A window.'

'For a moment I thought it was your head hitting off the desk.'

'As if.'*

The person to whom Thomas L'Estrange entrusted the proving of his brother-in-law's will, the person who oversaw the sale of Avonmore Lodge that July to Benjamin Courtney Hobson, was his partner Charles Henry Brett, who was himself the son of a Garrett (Martha, known as Matilda, wife of the Revd Wills Hill Brett of Greyabbey: the firm of L'Estrange and Brett had actually started life as Ramsey and Garrett for dear sake) and whose great-grandson Charles wrote the description of Warren Cottage for the Ulster Architectural Heritage Society and sat at a left diagonal to me during Thursday night Arts Council meetings.

It was a nice coincidence, but, sadly for me, nothing more. The succession of ownership had been entirely free of scandal. Besides, Henry John Garrett left an estate of close to six thousand pounds. My great-grandfather's had been little over six hundred pounds. It was still a sizeable amount, but not in the same league as the owners of Avonmore Lodge.

I reported all this to my father, who reported it to his brothers. A day or two later my father reported back to me. David in particular was adamant: the bet story was true and it did concern Avonmore. Hadn't their own Uncle David – the

* Cross my heart, verbatim. Besides, it is a criminal offence to tell a deliberate untruth in a work of non-fiction. Isn't it?

son, after all, of the man who had won and lost the house –
once taken him, when he was a boy of only seven or eight, on
a walk out along the Hillsborough Road and told him as they
passed the driveway up to Avonmore, 'That's where we
should have been'?

What is more, David reminded my father, who reminded
me, when David had started work as a trainee sales rep in
Lisburn at the age of sixteen, in the early 1940s, he regularly
met people, then in their late middle-age, who had clear
memories of seeing Eleanor around the town (less stately
galleon, more woman-of-war), remembered, some of them,
going into her shop in Smithfield, talking to her. In other
words, I might have cleared up the confusion over Eleanor's date
of birth with my work in the records offices and registries, but
there were certain inherited 'facts' that no amount of – or, for
that matter, no lack of – documentary evidence could gainsay.

I did not want to point out that David had also picked up in
these tyro years the claim that Eleanor had remarried, a man
called Davis: a butcher, David thought. Even my father and
Edmund had dismissed this as nonsense when David brought
it up the evening we met at my house. She had had an affair
with the man who ran one of the bars for her in east Belfast after
Phares died; that was all. (I wondered if it was wishful thinking
on David's part that this relationship had been in some way
solemnised.) And anyway I had been through the census
returns for 1901 and 1911 in which she was quite clearly
Eleanor Patterson, widow. I had seen her death certificate – her
headstone. She went to her grave a widow, and a Patterson.

For a few months I got on with other things. Eleanor, I
reminded myself, was not the focus of the book I was trying
to write. I had appointments to keep with her youngest son,

who had yet to experience the joys and the considerable complications of falling in love with my eventual grand-mother. There was a world war just over the horizon and, caught up with it, a more parochial but no less bitter conflict. There was (although I had admittedly set it myself) a dead-line for the delivery of the manuscript.

Then again, I had also discovered on my trip to Dublin that a parcel of land in Lisburn that I had always thought belonged to Phares and Eleanor had in fact been bought by the widow Eleanor in 1897. The land – four acres of it – lay off the far end of Antrim Street, where it became Antrim Road, and where Kate in the days when she used to stand on the doorstep greeting passers-by was in the habit of saying the 'big people' lived. Back in 1897 it was, or had been until recently, the town dump, and was being released now with approval for housing development: all in all not a bad way for a single woman with six children to invest some of her inheritance. Exactly a year later, however, Eleanor sold the four acres for the same price she had bought them to Hugh Kirkwood, who in a relatively short time had become one of the town's largest landowners and who modestly called one of the streets he proceeded to build on top of the dump 'Kirkwood's Road'.

Somewhere in the back of my mind in the months when the front of it was otherwise engaged this transaction niggled. Not a single penny profit. Eleanor.

Had she simply overstretched herself? The year 1897 also saw the final expansion of the shop into 37 Haslem's Lane, whose landlord, like number 39's, like 22 Smithfield's for that matter, was (niggle, niggle) Hugh Kirkwood.

Had she and Kirkwood been in secret compact all along, Eleanor – in return for more favourable terms in Haslem's

Lane, say – acting as a front for his continued acquisitions elsewhere in the town?

Had she suddenly needed money for some other business, or personal, project?

One Wednesday afternoon with an hour on my hands and these questions more insistent than usual – with an hour on my hands, the questions more insistent than usual *and* with a car parking space suddenly having presented itself as I drove along the street in question – I wandered into the Ulster Historical Foundation on College Square East in Belfast and on a whim tapped the name Eleanor Patterson (not Spence as I had hitherto) into their database of civil and religious marriages.* I found my great-grandmother eighth on a list of ten marriages. Her husband, Joseph Kelso Davis, was not a butcher, but a clerk, and a widower, with an address in Joy Street on the inner edge of Belfast city centre. His sister, Anne Hervey, who stood as witness for Eleanor, had lived in Lisburn before her own marriage, which suggested one possible connection. His late father, Jacob, had been a publican, which suggested a perhaps more compelling one.

Eleanor declares no occupation on the marriage certificate. She knocks off a couple more years than she is wont to from her age – the thirty-five she claims is only three years older

---

* 'Wandered' will do for my state of mind, but in truth you had to know what you were about to find your way into the Ulster Historical Foundation's College Square offices, through the door between Apache Tribe ('Clothing for Freaks') and the Scout Shop (more freaks!), up the all-too-authentic 1830s staircase to a landing presenting you with more doors than clues. The staircase remains, but the Foundation has removed to new, more welcoming premises on Waring Street, above a tapas bar and the Belfast Print Workshop. As long as you can find the right buzzer on the panel by the main entrance. How hard can it be to invent one of those things that you can actually read?

1899.	Marriage solemnised at *St Anne's* in the *parish* of *Belfast*					in the *Diocese of Connor*	
No.	When Married	Name and Surname	Age.	Condition.	Rank or Profession.	Residence at the Time of Marriage.	Father's Name and Surname.*	Rank or Profession of Father.*

| 72 | 24th May 1899 | Joseph Kilso Davis | 32 | Widower | Clerk | 83, Joy St Belfast | Jacob Davis | Publican |
| | | Eleanor Patterson *Minnie Spence* | 35 | Widow | — | 83 Woodstock Rd Ballymacarrett | Mitchell Spence | Farmer |

Married in the *Parish Church* according to the Rites and Ceremonies of the Church of Ireland, † *by Licence*, by me, *J Ernest Drury*

This Marriage was solemnised between us. *Joseph Kilso Davis* *Eleanor Patterson* in the Presence of us. *Robert Gamble* *Annie Finney*

* This information should be given whether the Fathers are living or dead, and if the names, &c., are not known, or if parties are unwilling to state them, a stroke should be drawn thus, ——— † "After Banns," "By Licence," &c., as the case may be.

than her husband – and, despite her lifelong Presbyterianism, describes herself as Church of Ireland, no doubt (displaying a pragmatism matched by her son a quarter of a century later) out of respect for the venue, Belfast's St Anne's Church, soon-to-be Cathedral. Well, I suppose if you are going to do Church of Ireland you might as well do it right.

She gives her own address as 83 Woodstock Road, Belfast.

My first thought, needless to say, was of my Uncle David. (My second was of the parking meter on College Square East, in case you thought I had floated out of the Ulster Historical Foundation without you noticing.) If he had been proved right about the marriage how could I ignore his insistence on the truth of the house story? How, come to that, had I so easily discounted the childhood memory he had related?

'That's where we should have been.'

Whether it was where I needed to be or not now, I could no longer keep away from Avonmore Lodge.

L'Estrange and Brett, it so happens, are among the largest depositors of papers in the Public Records Office of Northern

Ireland (PRONI). The archive, which stretches back to the middle of the nineteenth century and the eclipse of Ramsey and Garrett is, according to the PRONI website, 'staggering in its variety'. The index alone runs to ninety-three pages: testamentary papers, bankruptcy papers, liquidation papers, lunacy papers, papers concerning a debt of forty pounds (debtor thought to have emigrated to Africa, perhaps with the elusive Carlin), papers concerning sewer boundary disputes, disputes over the 'reasonable time of delivery' of a consignment of Belgian yarn, over the supply of 198 bags of flour, of a shipment of coal abandoned en route from Swansea; papers outlining malicious-injury claims, including one arising out of the destruction by fire of Annadale Hall, 'probably by suffragettes'*, papers accounting for the planting and sale of potatoes at one farm in Ballylesson during the Great Famine . . . And even then, as the introduction to the summary catalogue is at pains to point out, no attempt has been made to refer to *all* the papers in any given box.

The numbers on the boxes correspond to the numbered cubby-holes in the committee room of the firm's former

---

* Suffragettes, as it happens, were particularly active in Lisburn. In April 1914 an attempt was made to set fire to Castle House, formerly the residence of Sir Richard and Lady Wallace. More seriously still, in the early hours of 1st August, a bomb went off beneath one of the cathedral's stained-glass windows, breaking twenty-nine panes of glass. Four women were arrested in a nearby house. One of them, a Mrs Metge, had earlier in the summer tried to buy dynamite from a shop belonging to Hugh Kirkwood: to blow up a tree in her garden, she said. As they were being led from the courthouse following their arraignment the women were jostled by an angry mob. Windows were then broken in the house where they had been arrested. Mill girls were blamed, such behaviour clearly being beneath the majority of the good burghers of Lisburn. (Apologies, good burghers, I am setting you up here something rotten.)

offices in Chichester Street where the papers were stored for decades before being deposited in PRONI. The documents I requested – anything with a 'Hobson' or a 'Garrett' in the subject line – were spread over nine of these boxes, which were brought by trolley to my table in the reading room. Staggering is not the word. All the same I found the Avonmore Lodge papers without too much difficulty. There is much to be said for a numbered cubby-hole. In particular I found three drafts of the advertisement offering the house for sale by public auction at noon on Saturday 22nd July 1893. Benjamin Courtney Hobson's transition to the Lodge from Warren Cottage had not been the foregone conclusion I had assumed.

Pencilled notes on the back of the final draft of the sale bill detail the progress of the auction.

Lot one, the house, the lands attached (yearly rent thirty pounds) and the gate lodge, opened at four hundred pounds with a bid from Hobson, whose name is mistakenly written as Sinton throughout, and then amended, suggesting that his brother-in-law was bidding on his behalf, although perhaps not, in the light of future succession, entirely without self-interest. The next bid, one hundred pounds higher, came from a Mr Charley, the next, one hundred pounds higher again, from 'Mr Kirkwood'. Thereafter the hikes were not as dramatic and the bidding continued in its Hobson–Charley–Kirkwood sequence until Hobson's final bid of £815 went unanswered and the auctioneer brought his hammer down: Sold.

Lot two, Warren Cottage and lands, held under lease 'for the lives of their Royal Highnesses the Prince of Wales and Prince Alfred' at the yearly rent of sixteen pounds and ten shillings was bought unopposed by Hobson (or Sinton acting for Hobson) for two hundred pounds. Lot three, thirty acres of farmland adjoining Avonmore, was withdrawn without a single offer being made and, despite periodic re-advertising, was not finally disposed of until 1895.

Mr Kirkwood, it is safe to assume, is the ubiquitous Hugh. And Mr Charley? Well, the Charley family was another of those whose interests straddled linen and the law. Charleys already owned nine significant houses in the Lisburn hinterland, one of which, confusingly called Warren View, later Warren Cottage, near Derriaghy, was the home of John DeLorean when he arrived to deliver Northern Irish industry back to a prosperous future in the late 1970s with his fabulous gull-wing doors.* Fred Charley was one half of Charley & Allen, Phares and Eleanor's solicitors and, it transpires, Benjamin Courtney Hobson's too. Either Fred was bidding on his own behalf, against his client, or he was the legal representative of a man, Hobson, who was bidding against a Charley family relative. Or maybe there was a third possibility, that Fred like Sinton was bidding on someone else's behalf: another of his clients, say.

All at once Avonmore Lodge did not seem quite so far out of Phares and Eleanor's league. These were the types of people with whom they regularly had business dealings, people equally alive to the opportunities of the times. Like other solicitors in the town Charley & Allen were as ready to make loans as they were to chase debts: '£300 to lend, also £1,000 in sums to suit Borrowers, upon security of either Farms of Land or House Property at a reasonable rate of interest.'

---

* The house was repeatedly burgled during DeLorean's famously brief tenure after a rumour went around that he had had the bathroom fitted out with solid gold taps. (Robin Charley, 'Charley Family Houses in Dunmurry', in the journal of the Lisburn Historical Society, Volume 9, 1995.)

Given the frequency of ads such as this one from the *Lisburn Standard* of 24th February 1894 there cannot have been a shortage of takers, although to my early-twenty-first-century eyes the terms look a bit stark: repay or pack up.

In the week leading up to the auction of Avonmore Lodge Fred Charley was appearing in court in Lisburn 'on behalf of Mr Brett', trying to obtain repossession of the gate lodge from a man called Topping, who had been in the employ-ment of Henry Garrett and who had lived in the house for twenty-six years. Topping, through his solicitor, maintained that Brett, as executor and not landlord, had no right to evict him and claimed that he was in any event a freeholder whose occupation of the house was unconnected to his job. The case was held over until the week ending 19th August 1893 when, after a 'forcible speech' by Mr Allen, appearing on this occasion for Mr Brett, Topping was evicted.

Also before the court that week was a claim against Hugh Kirkwood for more than eleven hundred pounds in unpaid rent on his lands at Andersonstown, on the Lisburn side of west Belfast.

It is difficult to comprehend how anyone faced with even the remotest prospect of having to repay such a sum would a few days later bid as high as eight hundred pounds to buy another house, but while it is tempting to portray Kirkwood as a bit of a cowboy (if I can't get clarity, why not just add to the murk?) the truth is that the auction of Avonmore Lodge was conducted against a backdrop of widespread turmoil in landownership and tenancy. A land act two years previously had tried to refine the famous 1881 act, which had promised tenants the Three Fs: fair rents, fixity of tenure and free sale; but this further act still left room for grievance and confusion. The problem was put very succinctly at a meeting of tenant farmers – including more Pattersons and Dunwoodys than you could shake a blackthorn stick at – in the Masonic Hall at Cargycreevy on the very day in December 1894 that great-grandfather Phares died. (Maybe *that's* where Eleanor was when the enigmatic Charlotte was at her husband's bedside.) Under the current system, one speaker said, they were paying rent to hereditary landlords on what was for all practical purposes their own property. That was nothing short of robbery, and robbery, he needn't tell this audience, meant ruin.

In Lisburn, where all of this coincided with the death of Sir Richard Wallace, the 'benevolent baronet' of newspaper leader columns, a Wallace Tenants' Defence Association had been formed to support those in dispute with his widow, Lady Wallace.* In her own defence, it has to be said, Lady Wallace was trying her damnedest to offload as much of her land as possible. It was one of the reasons why Hugh Kirkwood was able to amass such an amount of property in the next few years.

These tenants' associations might have claimed they were concerned with moral as opposed to political rights, but there was a distinct and uncharacteristic militancy in some of their utterances. The local Conservative MP, for instance, had declined to attend the meeting in Cargycreevy Masonic Hall, and instead sent a letter in which he professed himself baffled that, as Unionists, the tenants could have any complaint against him. The chairman responded to its reading by

* She had been born Julie-Amélie-Charlotte Castelnau in 1819 and was working in a Paris perfumery when she became Sir Richard's mistress during the 1840s. She didn't become his wife until shortly before they fetched up in Lisburn for the first time. She never again returned to the town after her husband's death, but retired permanently to Hertford House in London: www.wallacecollection.org.

urging the meeting to adopt a resolution to return to parliament 'only such men as shall pledge themselves to faithfully represent us'.

Even as reported speech his words and the reaction to them are stirring:

> Any man who voted [in the House of Commons] against their just demands, let them vote against that man – (applause) – no matter who he might be, at the next general election; for the time had come when they must think for themselves and their families; and if they allowed themselves to be turned aside by any false issue they would deserve nothing but scorn and derision. (Applause.)

For 'false issue' it is impossible not to read Home Rule, or, since these were, as their MP had reminded them, Unionist tenant farmers, opposition to Home Rule. This had been the other big political story in Ireland in the previous few years and although the House of Lords had seen off the latest 'Betrayal Bill' (the *Lisburn Standard* nailing its true-blue colours firmly to the mast) the threat was still fresh enough in the memory to be expected to bring Protestant malcontents to heel. The expectation was reasonable, just a little premature.

Throw into this volatile mix of disputes and lawsuits a character of Phares's propensities – his track record of litigation – and it becomes less of an effort to believe that some incident of the kind passed down by his children to their children (and from them to me) might indeed have occurred.

Which is to admit, finally, that I never did get to the bottom of the Avonmore legend, unless of course my lawyer friend (my *first* lawyer friend) was right and the bottom line is that it is . . . well, *baseless*.

As luck would have it, though, I did, while trawling through the Lisburn newspapers for Kirkwoods and Hobsons and Bretts – anything resembling a Phares – stumble across one entirely unexpected name.

Back in July 1893, in the run-up to the auction, Fred Charley had one other piece of business in the town court on the day he moved to have Mr Topping evicted from the gate lodge. He applied to the bench for a protection order on behalf of Joseph Kelso Davis, in regard to the licensed premises in Smithfield formerly in possession of Henry Ashe. The applicant, said Mr Charley, had recently come into possession of that 'rather dilapidated' property, which had been held in trust until he attained his majority, that is, in 1893, turned twenty-five.

The connection between Eleanor and Joseph Kelso Davis turned out to have been very direct indeed. She had married the boy – and the bar – next door.

And Again?

Three weeks after the wedding, Eleanor accidentally killed Joseph Davis in the bedroom of 22 Smithfield and in her panic fed his dismembered body through the mincer in the store out the back of the shop . . .

Well I am damned if I can think what became of him if she didn't. The marriage certificate is the last documentary proof that the man ever existed and David's vague recollections aside he has left no trace whatever in the family history. Mind you he seems almost to pass in and out of Eleanor's life and memory as fast as the town dump passed through her hands. It is there plain as day on the 1901 census: 'Head of Household, Eleanor *Patterson*, widow.'

Looking again at this census, however, there appears to be a discrepancy between Eleanor's signature and her signature in 1911, a more significant discrepancy than might be accounted for by the mere passage of a decade. The suspicion that they were not made by the same person is reinforced by Jack's entry for 1901: 'John S.' Would Eleanor Clements Patterson have omitted or downplayed the 'C' she had inserted with such pride into her youngest son's name?

And, if the answer is no, is it possible that whoever did fill in the census was unaware of Eleanor's change in status or even her whereabouts?

The addresses that Eleanor and Joseph wrote beside their names in the register of St Anne's Church are almost certainly no more than addresses of convenience. Eleanor's '83 Woodstock Road' was a bar leased by William Crossley to Matthew McCusker, although you cannot rule out entirely that Eleanor had an interest in it somewhere along the line. Joy Street, where her groom claimed to be living, was so famous for its temporary lodgings and its associations with the nearby music halls that it had acquired the nickname the 'Street of the Three Ps' – (fuck your Fs) – 'Pride, Poverty and Pianos'.*

It is hard to understand why they should have needed to resort to such strategies. They were both widowed, there ought to have been no legal impediment to them marrying on their own terms, in their own town. If on the other hand the objections were social or familial it is equally difficult to see how the newly-weds could simply have returned to Lisburn and set up home together.

My father and his brothers had insisted to me on several occasions that their Uncle David had been running the family business – badly – and although he is only a grocer's assistant on the 1901 return he might well have been, at nineteen,

---

* This from p. 202 of Marcus Patton's *Central Belfast, A Historical Gazetteer* (UAHS, 1993): a book to get lost in. Charlie Chaplin lodged at 24 Joy Street in 1906 and again in 1907, which, Belfast being what Belfast is these days, I would have thought might have merited a festival of some sort. Belfast being what Belfast also is, next door, number 26, bears a plaque marking the spot where Joe McCann, an Official IRA folk hero, was shot by the British Army on 15th April 1972.

effectively (or ineffectively) in charge. What is certainly not in doubt is that Jack talked a lot to his sons about 'Auntie McNeill', Eleanor's sister Agnes, and how in his childhood she had seemed to be at Smithfield more often than she was at her own house, more often, by implication, than Eleanor herself was. The phrase 'like a mother to him' might have been coined for Auntie McNeill. She was so like a mother in fact that she shares a grave not with 'Uncle' McNeill, but with Eleanor and Phares, although – as in life so in death – her presence there below the ground is unacknowledged above.

Jack was six and a quarter in May 1899 when Eleanor remarried. He was on the register of Christ Church Infant School, or Nicholson Memorial as it was soon to become, a short walk down Barrack Street from Smithfield. His attendance in the school year about to end was 149 days out of a possible 210, or a shade under three-quarters. Not great, but not much different from the year before or the year after and certainly not bad enough to suggest that he had been out of range of the school for any length of time. That autumn he moved up to the elementary class, joining his brother Fred, then aged seven, and his sister Emma, who was ten. If, as seems possible, Eleanor was living away from 22 Smithfield during that year and the years immediately following, Jack was not with her. None of her children were.

And yet even then the anecdotal evidence is contradictory. Again my father and his brothers grew up with stories of musical evenings in the drawing room above the shop: no hint in these of discord or desertion. William, the eldest son, was an accomplished, and a versatile, musician, who played nine instruments (sequentially; he wasn't that versatile) and appeared at the Alhambra and Empire music halls in Belfast, on the same bill no doubt as some of the temporary residents of Joy Street, accompanying William James Ashcroft the 'Solid Man'.*

When British forces broke the Boer siege of Mafeking, after 217 days, in May 1900, bonfires were lit in Smithfield marketplace. William stood among them playing 'Goodbye Dolly Gray' and 'Comrades' on the cornet. It was his Lisburn swansong. Soon afterwards he married Dora Lavender (they just don't make names like that any more: I know, I've Googled it) and moved with her to Belfast – living at 18 Templemore Street to begin with – and that was the last that was heard of his cornet and his eight other instruments. He did, though, stay in the grocery line in a manner of speaking, becoming first a breadserver then, in time, a member of the Belfast Breadservers' Union. (There were 500 members. Truly, Dora Lavender, it was another world then.) In 1922 the Breadservers merged with the Transport and General Workers' Union (TGWU). William rose through the ranks, acquiring as he went such friends as Ernest Bevin – a TGWU leader before he became Minister for Labour and Foreign Secretary – and eventually settling in some style at

* 'Muldoon the Solid Man' had first been a vaudeville hit in the 1870s for Edward 'Ned' Harrigan, himself immortalised in the song 'Harrigan' by George M. Cohan, or at least by James Cagney as Cohan in *Yankee Doodle Dandy*, the film that, when I first saw it at the age of six or seven, put it into my head that I wanted to be a writer, *song* writer at any rate. At the launch of my first novel my Uncle David who had himself played the ukulele in a minstrel band in his teens told me that he always knew the talent would emerge again somewhere in the family line. For more on Harrigan see www.blarneystar.com. For more on me and Jimmy Cagney – because, I don't know, maybe life turned out to be not so short after all – see 'The BBC made me a deconstructionist and called it macaroni' in my book *Lapsed Protestant*.

Clarendon Street in Derry. As the oldest son of a widowed mother, however, even a mother who had subsequently remarried, William continued to exert considerable influence over the family: considerable and, despite his union activities, deeply conservative. In later years when his nephew, my own Uncle David, started worrying at the age gap between Eileen and himself, Uncle William told him in no uncertain terms to 'leave the past alone'.

William had stayed on at school beyond the normal leaving age of fourteen, attending what was then still the Lisburn Intermediate and University School, the future Wallace High. His younger sister Emma qualified as an elementary school teacher, teaching for a time in the same Nicholson Memorial School where she had been a pupil. Fred, although he left school at the earliest opportunity, took night classes in Inorganic Chemistry and Chemical Technology at the Technical College in Belfast in the course of his apprenticeship at the Glenmore Bleach Works: looking for the formula to make something more of himself.

Jack's school career is less certain. He was 'struck off' the Standard Six register at Nicholson Memorial on 16th March 1907, three weeks after his fourteenth birthday. (A lot less alarming than it sounds: everyone's schooldays ended with a 'striking off' then.) Four years later, however, in April 1911, he is listed on the census, the one that it appears Eleanor definitely did sign, as a 'scholar'. My Uncle David thinks he may in the interim have been attending Carrick Academy, a small, private business-school above a butcher's shop on Bow Street. (The academy actually extended across the archway leading into Haslem's Lane.) My cousin Ella, who of all the next generation down from David's spent most time with our grandparents, says that is the first she ever heard of it: his formal schooling ended at fourteen, of that she is certain. Another possibility, since 'scholar' on the census also covered young persons receiving instruction at home, is that Emma was tutoring her brother. She had finished teaching at Nicholson Memorial at the close of the 1909 school year and does not appear to have been formally employed thereafter, although she is still 'school teacher' on the census. At the very least – on this everyone is agreed – Jack acquired from her a more-than-elementary knowledge of French.

Despite the turmoil of his early childhood, the impression is of a young man raised to a degree of refinement (these were the days of the Choral Society and musical arrangements), even indulgence. Which is not to say he hadn't inherited a bit of horse sense too. In the spring of 1910 he walked into R. J. Allen's second-hand shop on Bridge Street and asked about a concert flute in the window display that had caught his eye.

The price tag said a guinea. 'Yes, but how much is it really?' he asked the owner.

'A guinea.'

Jack left the shop without the flute, but came back the following week and asked again. He came back, in fact, four weeks in a row (I can just see R. J. Allen's face) until he had bargained the price down by a florin to nineteen shillings.*

* My father inherited both the facility for the flute and the haggling, but passed only the latter on to me, and even then not terribly successfully. I preface all requests for money off with 'My dad's a Lisburn man and wouldn't forgive me if I didn't ask.' Once, in a picture-framer's (a picture-framer's! Have I no shame?) the owner countered she was a Lisburn woman too – knew my father and grandparents well. She didn't give me a single penny discount.

However long she had been absent in the end in the wake of her second marriage it is impossible not to sense Eleanor's presence in 22 Smithfield at this juncture. Phares's reckless-ness and her son David's inexperience may have damaged the family business, she may even have allowed herself to be distracted from it for a time, but she still had aspirations and ambitions. During the course of 1911, Jack's scholar days finally came to an end when he was apprenticed to William J. Gillespie of Bow Street, House Furnisher, Ironmonger, Hardware Merchant, and Purveyor of Fancy Goods ('only first-class workmen employed'), with a view, it seems, to diversifying out of groceries and bags of meal and into sideboards and chiffoniers.

And talking of outs and ins . . .

David, who married in 1909 (the less fragrant-sounding Mary Bowman), had followed William out of Smithfield and into breadserving. Within a year, though, he and his wife were in a shop of their own on the busy Lisburn Road, about a mile from Belfast city centre. In his absence his sister Agnes –

Aggie to the family — was acting as Eleanor's assistant. Also residing above the shop at this time, but most definitely not assisting in it, was the future Mrs Isabella P. Horn, then in her early twenties, whose occupation on the census of 1911 is listed as 'private'.

She was still there a year and a half later on 28th September 1912, 'Ulster Day', when she walked across Smithfield to the Grain Market on Market Place and signed the women's Declaration in support of the Solemn League and Covenant against Home Rule for Ireland:

> We whose names are underwritten, women of Ulster, and loyal subjects of our gracious King, being firmly persuaded that Home Rule would be disastrous to our Country, desire to associate ourselves with the men of Ulster in their uncompromising opposition to the Home Rule Bill now before Parliament, whereby it is proposed to drive Ulster out of her cherished place in the constitution of the United Kingdom, and to place her under the domination and control of a Parliament in Ireland. Praying that from this calamity God will save Ireland, we hereto subscribe our names.

Eleanor added her name to the Declaration too, although she preferred to do it in Lisburn First Presbyterian Church (a reconciliation after her dalliance with the Episcopalians?), one of three venues besides the Grain Market open to cope with the expected demand that day.

I was brought up believing that Jack had signed the Covenant as well: in his own blood, even. I remember repeating that last detail proudly to my friends in the days when

Covenants and blood meant something to me.* The 'own blood', however, turns out to be a popular myth. Only one of the 471,414 signatories of Covenant and Declaration – Major Fred Crawford, of whom more presently – is believed to have opened a vein for his name. Still, I would tell you, hand on heart (there is clearly a bit of the covenanter in me yet), that after my grandfather's death I saw hanging in my Uncle Jackie's house the souvenir parchment Covenant with which each signatory was presented. Jackie is dead now too and the whereabouts of what was in his house is a matter of some debate, not to say friction. Practically the first thing I did, though, when I started this book was consult the online Ulster Covenant database hosted by the Public Records Office, but I have been through the Pattersons a dozen times (there are 2,300 of them), I have looked under Jack, John, John C., John S., John S. C., John Samuel, John Samuel Clements; I have looked under every conceivable misspelling (Eleanor C. was incorrectly transcribed into the database as Eleanore L.). I have not found my grandfather.

There had been a major torch-lit rally in Lisburn on the night of 19th September 1912, the day that the text of the Covenant was first made public. (It had been awaited it seems like the final instalment of *The Old Curiosity Shop*.) Large numbers of men marched shouldering dummy rifles. *The Times* likened the throng to 'the sea with a storm brooding over it'.† For many

* Robert McLiam Wilson in *Ripley Bogle* has the Ulster Protestant girls of his hero's youth plaster their bedroom walls with pictures of Oliver Cromwell. He is joking, of course. John Pym was the pin-up.

† I am quoting from p. 63 of *The Ulster Crisis* (Faber, 1969) by A. T. Q. Stewart, who is in turn quoting from Ian Colvin's *The Life of Lord Carson* (Gollancz, 1935). I suppose one of us should have gone and looked at the actual newspaper. I suppose he will say it should have been me.

people watching this would have been the first direct evidence of organised resistance to the third Home Rule Bill, although there had been meetings and mass rallies aplenty in the previous six months. In his diary for 1960 Jack records below the week ending 9th April, 'Anti Home Rule demonstration at Balmoral Show Grounds 9th April 1912. Attendance estimated at 100,000 from as far as Limerick. LCFB present.' LCFB stands for Lisburn Conservative Flute Band. Also present was the leader of the Conservative Party, then in opposition, Andrew Bonar Law, who a few months earlier had declared, apropos of the government's plans for Ulster, that there were things stronger than parliamentary majorities.

At Balmoral that day he and Jack and a hundred thousand others witnessed the unfurling of the world's largest Union Jack. (I don't know, had they regular giant Union Jack competitions in those days?)*

By the turn of 1913 the resistance had become more organised still with the formation of the Ulster Volunteer Force, which at its height numbered fifty thousand men, about one in ten of the adult male population, or, since membership was restricted to signatories of the Covenant, one in four of those eligible to join – closer to one in two of those of military age.

This was the culmination of a conflict that had been threatening for almost thirty years, since the then Liberal Prime Minister William Gladstone had first declared it his intention – his mission – to bring about self-government in

---

* Jack returned to Balmoral in April 1962 for the fiftieth anniversary of the rally. I was there too, aged eight months, with my parents and older brothers. Maybe in April 2012, for old times' sake . . . Or maybe not.

Ireland. The Home Rule (aka 'Betrayal') Bill thrown out by the House of Lords in 1893 had followed one seven years earlier that had failed even to make it out of the lower house. When the Lords rejected the next Liberal government's budget in 1909, however, an election was called, as a result of which the Irish Nationalists held the balance of power. The Liberals' main aim was to curtail the Lords, so that in future they would not be able to block bills that had already been passed by the Commons. As part of the deal for the Nationalists' support one of the first pieces of legislation to be introduced when parliament reconvened was another Home Rule Bill. The Commons eventually passed the bill at the close of 1912. The Lords duly rejected it, but under the new Parliament Act they could only delay its becoming law.

Opposition to Home Rule was concentrated in Ulster, although the leader of Unionism in Ireland since 1910 was the Dublin-born barrister, and scourge of Oscar Wilde, Edward Carson. (He was born in fact within half a mile, and a mere eight months ahead, of Wilde.) As the crisis deepened and the mood of confrontation spread there was talk of all-out civil war. In the south of the country a Nationalist Irish Volunteer Force was formed in imitation – admiration, almost – of the Ulster Volunteers. Its secretary was Bulmer Hobson, educated at Friends' School Lisburn. Like many of his fellow Volunteer leaders Hobson was also a member of the clandestine Irish Republican Brotherhood, or IRB.*

In the north especially, religious tension increased.

---

* As the name suggests, Friends' was originally a Quaker school. I am assuming a connection somewhere not too far down the line between Bulmer and Benjamin Courtney Hobson, but – I am thinking of you, Reader – I am not going to force it.

Lisburn had seen some sectarian disturbances in the closing decades of the nineteenth century, mostly around the Sacred Heart of Mary Convent on Castle Street, on one occasion after schoolchildren had been heard singing patriotic songs on St Patrick's Day. (Imagine, the *neck* on them: patriotic songs on St Patrick's Day!) For the most part, though, the town had been free of the riots that regularly erupted in Belfast, where Catholics and Protestants were more evenly matched. An outgoing police commander boasted, as late as spring 1920, that there had never been so much as a baton charge in the town.

Henry Bayly, in his 1834 *Topographical & Historical Account of Lisburn*, attributed the relative calm to the good behaviour of the town's Catholics:

> Whatever be the cause, this sect of Christians residing here, (and indeed in the surrounding districts,) have always been remarkable for their peaceable conduct and moral behaviour, being greatly divested of that antipathy to Protestants, and that bigotry and intolerance which distinguish those of Dublin, Cork, and other large cities.*

Presumably being thus divested they would have understood why a Protestant townswoman should want one of their number to hand another Protestant title deeds on the town-hall steps.

---

* Bayly is similarly 'charitable' to the Quakers, whose views he decides are 'perfectly consonant to the spirit of Christianity', before noting less ambiguously, 'It will reflect eternal credit on the Quakers of Ireland that from them issued the first censure, passed by any public body [the year was 1727], on that abominable traffic, the SLAVE TRADE.'

The Other Side

Mary Jane McKeaveny had grown up in rural Hillhall, a mile and a half over the other, County Down, side of the River Lagan from Lisburn town centre, along what I still think of as the 'back road' to Belfast. She married Daniel Logue on 10th October 1878 when both were barely out of their teens. She was a Presbyterian, he was a Catholic, the son of William, a Lisburn butcher, and Margaret Logue, who lost four of her five children before she herself died, aged thirty-seven, in 1872. Thirty years before the *Ne Temere* decree though it was, the wedding, in a triumph of faith over tradition, took place in his church, St Patrick's on Chapel Hill, not hers. They were living on Murdoch's Row when Kate was born in the summer of 1894, the seventh of ten children. (Eliza Jane, Margaret, Charlotte, John, Daniel and Mary had got there ahead of her; Thomas, William and Arthur came after. Oh, and I checked the weather, just in case. It was a peach of a day.) Most of their married lives, however, Daniel and Mary Jane spent in 44 Chapel Hill, almost directly opposite St Patrick's.

The first Catholic Church on the site had been completed in 1786, thanks, as an inscription above the door attested, to 'donations from people of every religion in the country'. By coincidence – or then again not – at almost the same time Protestants in Belfast were raising money for the building of a new 'Mass-house' there. The 1st Belfast Volunteer Company even provided a guard of honour for the priest on the opening of the chapel in May 1784.*

Chapel Hill at the tail end of the eighteenth century was, says Henry Bayly, a 'retired part of town'. By the time Daniel and Mary Jane Logue were raising their family there it was, while still on the edge, one of the most populous parts. Getting on for two-thirds of their three hundred neighbours on the street were, by birth or marriage, Catholic too. Most of the rest were Church of Ireland, including the family of Stewart and Mary Jane Wylie, who in 1901 were living at number 14. The eldest son, John Wylie, is the man whose address in Bangor is among the earliest entries in Jack's 1970 diary.

The fairies at the bottom of the garden that Kate told her children about might have danced into her imagination from the Fairy Mount, or mound, in a field out the back of the chapel, although the Mount's name seems to have derived, rather prosaically, from a certain Neil Fairy who rented land here from the third Marquis of Hertford in 1829. (A better question might be where Neil Fairy's name derives from.)†

* Marcus Patton again: *Central Belfast Gazetteer*. Prior to that May the town's Catholics had met in a house in what is now College Court, but was then, gloriously and more aptly given the dimensions of the thoroughfare, Squeeze-gut Entry.

† Fred Kee, *Lisburn Miscellany*. Kee was Public Health Inspector in Lisburn from 1928 to 1982, and during the first half of the 1970s   *cont'd over/*

Kate's eldest sister, Eliza Jane, who had married – a Protestant, Harry Anderson – when Kate was only eight, lived in
a house in the adjacent Fairymount Square. And if that was
not enough to give her ideas, Kate too was often called the
'Wee Fairy'. As a child her hair was blonde and in ringlets.
She would tell you it herself, or at least she told my cousin
Ella: when she was young she was beautiful.

School made little impression and in any case was only ever
leading to one place. Already at the age of eleven she was a
'half-timer' at the Barbour Threads Mill in Hilden. By
fourteen she was working there full-time. Her walk to
and from work – a distance of just over a mile – would
have taken her right through the centre of town: Chapel Hill,
Bow Street, Market Square, Castle Street, Seymour Street,
Wesley Street, the Low Road. She and her friends sang all the
way, arms linked the width of the footpath. It is at once a
picture of innocence and an image to fill teenage boys with
dread (and often something more than dread), even now, long
after the mills have become civic centres and artists' studios
and luxury apartment blocks, and the term 'millies' has
floated free of its origins to settle like a slur on any group
of self-possessed, footpath-hogging, working-class girls.

Who knows how many times Kate and her friends passed
Jack on the street – how many times they caused him to step

---

† *cont'd*   published articles in the *Ulster Star* on many of the streets and
entries his job had taken him to. In the preface to the book that these articles
eventually became he thanked 'all those worthy citizens of Lisburn who
contributed knowingly or unknowingly to the contents'. One of those who
did so knowingly was Jack. Kee was a regular caller at Antrim Street (*more
coal on there, Jack*) and, as my father tells it, was given 'stacks' of papers on his
visits. You can guess what I am thinking: maybe the legs the Avonmore
papers acquired were Fred's . . . But Fred's dead, people. Fred's dead.

off the footpath and into the street – before he noticed her, or she him. Who knows how many times she passed under Eleanor's disapproving gaze (not only were they millies, they were Chapel Hill millies), neither of them guessing that their lives were destined to become intertwined.

But not just yet.

For entertainment the girlfriends went to dances in the 'Wee Hall', a former Methodist chapel converted – in more senses than one – by the Ancient Order of Hibernians and standing next to the blacksmith's forge at the corner of Linenhall Street and Smithfield. (The 'Big Hall', St Joseph's, was up on Chapel Hill.) In later years the dances at the Wee Hall would become much more exclusively Catholic in complexion, but for the time being they were just another place for all the young people of the town to go. I look at the distance, which is no distance at all, from the corner of Haslem's Lane to the corner of Linenhall Street and I feel my grandparents spinning closer and closer. If only she would let go of all those other girls' arms . . .*

Kate's brother Billy, who never married, would lead off the dances with his friend Hughie McClinton. That was as much as you said in those days: 'never married' and 'led off with his friend'. Billy lived for many years with his elder brother Tommy, who did marry eventually, in his sixties, much to everyone's surprise, his own, I suspect, included. Another brother, Dan, played Irish League football for Distillery. The club's Grosvenor Park stadium was on the edge of Belfast's

---

* Appropriately enough the Wee Hall was officially opened by 'Wee' Joe Devlin, the Belfast Nationalist leader and MP for the west of the city. Devlin was a long-time president of the Hibernians: some even credit him with founding the modern order, although organisations using that name had existed since the seventeenth century. (CAIN website: marching orders.)

Lower Falls, which is possibly how Dan met his wife-to-be, Margaret Aughy, who lived in nearby Leeson Street. The two were married in the spring of 1913 in the same St Anne's Church where Eleanor had married Joseph Kelso Davis fourteen years earlier. For the purposes of the certificate at least, Dan gave an address on Athol Street, at the city end of the Grosvenor Road, and his religion as Church of Ireland. The ceremony was conducted by the Revd Frederick Herbert Paget L'Estrange (I will not go there; I will not go there), described by one organist who played under him (or there) as 'a solid High Churchman . . . an Irish Nationalist at heart and Catholic to the core'.*

And if there is a better expression of the agreeable fuckedupness of faith and politics in this part of the world than a Catholic passing himself off as a Protestant in order to be married by a Protestant who is deep down a Catholic I can't think of it: 'World is crazier,' as the poet says, 'and more of it than we think, Incorrigibly plural.'†

---

* The organist in question was Billy Adair, the occasion, as I'm sure you know, an address given in 2003 to the Ulster Society of Organists and Choirmasters. Distillery were forced out of Grosvenor Park in July 1971 due to the worsening sectarian violence in the area. They shared seven different grounds in the next ten years before moving to a dog track at Ballyskeagh, near Lambeg, and becoming Lisburn Distillery.

† Louis MacNeice, 'Snow'. L'Estrange was for a time rector of Carrowdore Church, where MacNeice's ashes are interred, or depending on who you believe the ashes of his friends George and Mercy Hunter's umbrella stand, MacNeice's own ashes having been accidentally left in the George pub (no relation), round the corner from the BBC on Portland Place. MacNeice's father, Revd John MacNeice, was, like L'Estrange, Nationalist in his political sympathies, but was nevertheless required as Bishop of Down, Connor and Dromore to preach at the funeral of Sir Edward – by the time of his death *Lord* – Carson in October 1935. ('Snow' had been written, apparently, in the Bishop's Malone Road residence the previous January.) The Bishop did insist on one point of principle, refusing to allow the Union flag to be flown above the grave in St Anne's Cathedral.

There were two weddings in the Patterson family that same
year. On 4th October Emma married James Moneypenny at
Willowfield Parish Church on the Woodstock Road, strength-
ening the east Belfast connection. Less than four weeks later,
on the morning of Hallowe'en, her elder sister Aggie married
Lawrence Hannon*, who hailed from Derrymacash in County
Armagh but worked in Lisburn as a barman (was there a
pattern here, a genetic predisposition?) at Dan Mooney's on
Chapel Hill. This second wedding took place in Ardoyne,
north Belfast, at Holy Cross Roman Catholic Church. Once
again it is not immediately apparent why the marriage should
have been celebrated in a church to which neither bride nor
groom was connected by residence or birth. Or at least the
most obvious reason is called into question by the fact that
both give their address on the marriage certificate as 22
Smithfield. (It is considered worthy of repetition in the
Comment column after the officiating priest's name.) You
cannot entirely rule this out as yet another address of convenience – although why bother with one that lay outside the
parish concerned? Neither, though, can you rule out the
possibility that Eleanor's bark was sometimes worse than
her bite and that her contempt for 'Papishes' was more general
than particular. So much a part of the family was Lawrence
Hannon that Jack, who at this stage, a decade before his
rendezvous with W. P. Nicholson, displayed some of his
father's characteristics and tastes, would travel with him
regularly to race meetings in England and Scotland.

* I use the spelling on his marriage certificate, although everyone I spoke to
pronounced it 'Hennan'. McKenny's Bar, likewise, on p. 32, was pronounced 'McKinney's'. I took the spelling I have used from a newspaper
report: a glowing reference, alas. (Alas? Alas.)

Besides, if Aggie had been banished who would have been left to help Eleanor out in the shop?

All this time the Home Rule crisis was deepening. Throughout 1913 efforts had been made to import guns to arm the UVF, the vast majority of them co-ordinated by Major Fred 'Signed in Blood' Crawford. In one cunning ruse he put on an American accent to buy six Maxim machine guns from an arms manufacturer in London. (In the dupe's defence, I suppose, Hollywood movies were still in their infancy, still silent, and the gentleman enquiring about the Maxims did say he was called John *Washington* Graham. What could be more American than that?)* It was Crawford who proposed to the Ulster Unionist Council – effectively an independent government-in-waiting – a 'big run' to bring in thousands of guns in one fell swoop; and it was Crawford, reprising his role as J. W. Graham, who went to Hamburg to buy them. They were landed at Larne, on the east Antrim coast, on the night of 24th April 1914 and dispatched under cover of darkness to UVF units throughout Ulster. The news broke the following day, which also happened to be the day that Burnley beat Liverpool before King George V in the final of the FA Cup at Crystal Palace. The *Daily Express* headline on Monday ran the two events together. 'Coup Final', it said.

Ten weeks earlier, on Valentine's Day 1914, John Milne Barbour, chairman of Barbour Threads, reputed to be the world's largest linen-thread mill, the mill to which Kate and her friends walked singing every day, laid the foundation stone for a new Orange Hall at Derriaghy, two miles out

* Stewart, *The Ulster Crisis*, p. 88. See also the 'Operation Lion' chapter for subsequent Crawford exploits.

along the Belfast Road from Lisburn and about five hundred
yards from his own home, Conway House. As the name
suggests, Conway House had once belonged to the
descendants of Sir Fulke, and while the Barbour family's own
association with Lisburn was not quite as venerable it was
arguably every bit as significant. They had leased their first
bleaching green in the town at the end of the eighteenth
century and when the mill at Hilden finally closed its doors
in 2006 it brought to an end 222 years' continuous production. The plant manager at the time told the *Ulster Star*,
'Barbour's history is Lisburn's history.'*

Among the speakers in the build-up to the stone-laying was
Brother E. J. Charley JP, 'worshipful master' of Loyal Orange
Lodge 135, who made reference in his speech to a marked
increase in membership of the Order, especially among the
young. It had, he said, always been so in critical days.

And Brother Charley (the E was for Edward, the J for
Johnston, but his friends all knew him as Eddie) spoke with
some authority on the matter. A close relative of Fred
Charley, the Lisburn solicitor, his forebears had come to
Ulster from Lancashire, where they had a reputation as
Jacobites. Having prospered in the Belfast linen trade, in
1727 they bought a twelve-bedroom house at Ballyfinaghy –
Finaghy for short – midway between Belfast and Lisburn.
From this base in the decades that followed the Charleys
spread out into the network of big houses previously referred

* Barbour's history also cut across Belfast's history – and Hollywood's. John
Milne's sister was married to Thomas Andrews, who as head of draughting at
Harland and Wolff helped design the *Titanic* and went down with it on its
maiden voyage in April 1912. She later married Henry Harland, a nephew of
Sir Edward Harland, the shipyard's founder. Where she was on Valentine's
Day 1914, however, I cannot say.

to and into a number of other areas of influence, most notably the Orange Order, about as far from their Jacobite heritage as it is possible to imagine. The field to which the Twelfth of July parade had been making its way each year since the mid-nineteenth century was on the Charleys' Finaghy land. The Bible that was read from in the religious service at the field was – the sole stipulation for the use of the land – a Charley family Bible.

By the time I was growing up, in Finaghy, in the 1960s, Finaghy House had become Faith House, an old-people's home run by the Brethren. A fifteen-foot-high wire fence separated the gardens from the swing park on the edge of the housing estate where I lived. So of course one of our great dares – as though old age was a disease you could catch if you got too close* – was to scale the fence or, for the fainter of heart, burrow underneath it.

A short walk from the park, my primary school sprawled like an American suburb on still another Charley bequest, or so I know now, having been asked a couple of years back to write a foreword for the Finaghy Friendship Group's *Finaghy Life* book. More than write a foreword, I was invited to speak at the launch in the school itself. I had thought it would be nice to read from an autobiographical piece about playing the Lord Chancellor in the school's production of *Iolanthe* ('The law is the true embodiment. Of everything that's excellent. It has no kind of fault or flaw, And *I*, my Lords, embody the law'), summer term 1973, while beyond the school gates Belfast erupted: read it in the very assembly hall where that production was staged. The assembly hall, though, had gone, or at least been relocated, to roughly where the swimming pool was in my day. Don't ask me what had become of the

* It was, the symptoms were just a bit slower manifesting themselves than we had been expecting; slower and all the more pernicious for that.

swimming pool. Of the school I attended, more or less all that remained was the name, and the gates.

The last Twelfth parade to Finaghy Field was in 1972 (because Finaghy, like just about everywhere else in the city, had suddenly discovered that it had two sides, with the Field marooned on the 'wrong' one), eleven months before our *Iolanthe*, four months after the proroguing of Stormont and the introduction of Direct Rule from Westminster to a Northern Ireland that did not even exist when the foundation stone of Derriaghy Orange Hall was laid in February 1914.*

The hall was officially opened by Edward Charley's niece on Saturday 4th July. Most of the town's Orange lodges paraded from Lisburn for the ceremony, accompanied as ever by bands, among them Lisburn Conservative with Jack on his nineteen-shilling flute. Proceedings began with a resolution mourning the loss of Joseph Chamberlain, MP for Birmingham, who had died two days earlier and who together with his son Austen had been a long-time champion of the anti-Home Rule cause. Later another resolution was carried, with cheers, to follow Sir Edward Carson wherever he would lead. This was six days after the assassination in Sarajevo of Archduke Franz Ferdinand. In little over a month the (barely) United Kingdom was at war with Germany – destination of course for Major Fred Crawford's recent shopping trip – and Home Rule had been shelved for the duration. Carson, who had been on the verge of setting up a provisional government in Belfast, found himself instead appointed to the coalition government in London as attorney-general.

---

* John Milne Barbour, as Sir Milne, would serve as Minister for Finance in Stormont, succeeding his sister's brother-in-law by her first marriage, John Miller Andrews, who in turn became prime minister.

Almost overnight the 1st (Lisburn) Battalion of the South
Antrim UVF morphed into the 11th Battalion, the Royal
Irish Rifles, although 'almost' was not fast enough for some.
When the South Antrim regimental commander Colonel
Pakenham briefed a UVF parade on arrangements for en-
listment at the start of September he was informed that 'a
large number, rather than wait, had joined other regiments so
as to get away to the front as soon as possible'. In fact by the
time this report appeared in the *Lisburn Standard* on 11th
September, one Lisburn man, Private William Johnston, had
already been killed (on Wednesday 9th September) while
fighting on the Marne, east of Meaux, with the Duke of
Cornwall's Light Infantry regiment. Among the casualties in
the next four and a bit years was Edward Charley's youngest
sister, Maude Baily, who had married in Los Angeles but
returned at the outbreak of the war (it coincided with her
husband's death) to join the Dunmurry Voluntary Aid
Detachment. She died at the Thirty-eighth Stationary Hospital, Genoa, in September 1918, six months after another
sister's son, Captain Charles Francis Duffin, was killed in
France.*

At another ceremony in the autumn of 1914, in the
Salvation Army hall (rebuilt after the storms of 1894), each
UVF member enlisting in the newly constituted 36th Ulster
Division was presented with a replica of the button worn by
the Volunteers of an earlier era, the Lisburn Loyal Infantry,
who had been formed to resist invasion by a foreign power

* For these and all subsequent references to casualties – indeed for pretty
much anything you could want to know about the impact of the war on the
town – see the magnificent Friends' School Lisburn World War I Archive,
www.friendsschoollisburn.org.uk.

and who had, in a reversal of present circumstances, ended up fighting their fellow Irishmen. A painting of these Volunteers drilling in Market Square was on proud display in the foyer of the new Municipal Technical College – the old Castle House – although as a reminder that the reversal just mentioned (and the symbolism of the button) was far from neat the painting featured Henry Munro, who led that faction of the Volunteers which sided with the United Irishmen and whose head as a result wound up stuck on a pike in the same Market Square.

Jack, despite his attendance at rallies, his musical accompaniments, joined neither the UVF nor the 36th Ulster Division, but carried on serving his time at William J. Gillespie's on Bow Street. (Conscription was a non-starter for Ireland. Conscription in Ireland would have sparked another war.) Of the four military-age Patterson brothers, indeed, only one, Fred, went into uniform. And even he got no nearer to Flanders than Falkirk. Discharge papers from September 1916 record that Private Frederick Patterson (flummoxed again by Phares) was found permanently unfit by the medical board at Stirling after 270 days in the Army Reserve, Class B. Earlier that same year Kate's brother-in-law, her sister Maggie's husband Tommy O'Neill, was killed in action in France at the age of thirty-nine. He had re-enlisted in 1914 after an earlier stint in the Boer War, where he was awarded the King Edward Medal with three clasps. That's one clasp for each of the children he left, all under six.

I cannot imagine what it must have been like to be an apparently medically fit twenty-one-year-old going about your day-to-day business when so many of your peers were signing up to fight, which is not at all to say that I can imagine myself either rushing off to the recruiting office.

Even at a distance of a century the pressure is palpable from every page of the local papers where scarcely a week passes without a poem like 'Fill up the Gaps' ('you are all very loyal when it comes to talk and cheers . . . yet we'd think more about you/ If you assist us chaps/ And show no cause to doubt you/ If you fill up the gaps'), and other more artful appeals to the conscience:

And then there were the near constant reports of those Lisburn men risking limb, liberty, life itself, at the front: Private Patrick Furfey, a well-known cross-country runner of Old Hillsborough Road, killed in action at Ypres on 27th October 1914; Captain E. S. B. Hamilton, taken prisoner in the retreat from Mons in September; Private James Totten of Antrim Street, frostbitten in France as the winter set in, but 'doing splendidly' and hoping to be able soon to rejoin his battalion.

Sergeant G. Ruddock, serving with the 2nd South Lancashire regiment, wrote to the *Lisburn Standard* in December thanking Mrs George H. Clarke (weren't there a lot of mannish-sounding women's names too though in the olden times . . .) and through her all the people of Lisburn, who had raised £500 for a motor ambulance, 'Although I hope to be spared the doubtful pleasure of a journey in the conveyance in question.'

(He would indeed seem to have been spared, unlike Private Totten, who rejoined his battalion only to die of wounds on the Somme on 3rd July 1916, five months after the *Standard* reported him singing 'Where are the Boys of Antrim Lane?' in a concert in a frontline dugout.)

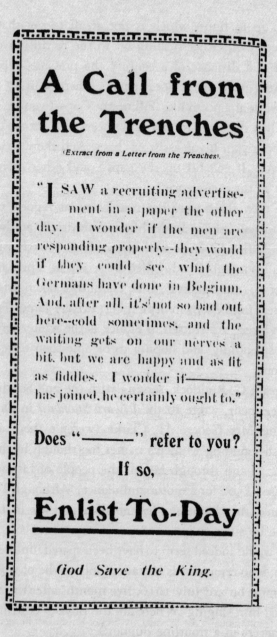

A Call from the Trenches

(Extract from a Letter from the Trenches).

" I SAW a recruiting advertisement in a paper the other day. I wonder if the men are responding properly--they would if they could see what the Germans have done in Belgium. And, after all, it's not so bad out here--cold sometimes, and the waiting gets on our nerves a bit, but we are happy and as fit as fiddles. I wonder if———— has joined, he certainly ought to."

Does "————" refer to you?

If so,

Enlist To-Day

God Save the King.

In the same issue as Sergeant Ruddock's letter an editorial urged Christmas cards for the boys in France and Flanders, but asked its readers not to send caricatures of the Kaiser, for fear of reprisals if their loved ones were captured with the caricatures about their person. The paper offered as an alternative its own *Lisburn Standard* range of 'all-British private greeting cards' to send to the troops. In the same civic-minded spirit, Beckett Bros. of Bow Street were advising citizens of Lisburn to thwart the Germans, whose recent surprise naval bombardment of Hartlepool, Scarborough, and Whitby had left more than a hundred dead, and give their friends Christmas presents as usual: really useful and sensible presents, of the sort Beckett Bros. stocked.*

Elsewhere the undiluted Christmas spirit was in even shorter supply. At the last scheduled meeting of the Lisburn Board of Guardians before the festivities a bitter row broke out over the suitability in these straitened times of the traditional 'Christmas Extras' for inmates of the workhouse, which had cost the town's rate-payers eleven pounds nine shillings and four pence the year before. After all, said one board member, the inmates had food, clothing, beds to sleep in: they were better off than the men in the trenches. A motion was passed withdrawing the extras, along with the

---

* The *Standard* also printed a French phrasebook, compiled by Mr Moran of Bridge Street, previously eighteen years resident in Brussels: 'The perfect French pronunciation given therein will enable every smart soldier possessing this very useful book to speak French in a week . . . [and] also prevent the British soldier from falling into the enemy lines if he should become detached from his regiment on the battlefield.' You have to feel for soldiers from other towns in Britain and Ireland, wandering lost and tongue-tied through German-held territory with pictures of Kaiser Bill in their pockets, his exaggerated moustaches turned up parallel with his nose.

shilling bonus normally paid to those in receipt of outdoor relief. Rather more sympathy, and money, was forthcoming later in the meeting when seven pounds and eight shillings was voted to compensate the supplier of sugar to the work-house for the sudden jump in wholesale price brought on by the war, although I am honour-bound to say that the Board met again in emergency session, days later, and reversed its decision on the Christmas Extras. Damn you, honour! Have you no concern at all for story?

To add to the air of beleaguerment, the town was still struggling to get on top of a scarlatina epidemic, which had closed schools for most of the month leading up to the holiday. (Given Lisburn's luck with fires it is probably fortunate that penicillin had just about dislodged the old cure of burning the possessions of scarlet-fever sufferers.) All the same it was the season to at least make a stab at being jolly, fa-la-la, fa-la-la, fa-la-la . . . For those who could overcome the fear of contagion and afford the three-pence in (although jam jars in this instance were also legal tender), the Picture House on Market Street had special Christmas Day and Boxing Day matinées of *The Chasm*: 'a dramatic story of a woman's sacrifice that turned to love', starring Gerda Holmes, Richard C. Travers, and the astonishing Bryant Washburn, who at the age of twenty-five had already appeared in more than fifty films.* Across the road at the

* His first, in 1911, was *The New Manager*, which was swiftly followed by *The Burglarized Burglar*. His final two films, in 1947, *Do or Diet* (thirty-six years and still the dodgy titles) and *Sweet Genevieve*, were his 324th and 325th, although from his appearance as Washed-up Star Telephoning in Brown Derby – a part you feel he was born to play – in the 220th, *What Price Hollywood?* (1932), his roles were as often as not uncredited, even (*For Me and My Gal*, 1942) unconfirmed. (See www.imdb.com.)

Electric Picture Palace (it was a veritable Shaftesbury Avenue, Market Street), aka the Orange Hall, Tom Gregory, 'comedian and expert dancer' was showcasing his 'quick-change' dancing. (Beats me too.) Those other expert dancers and novelty entertainers the Three Brightons would see out the Old Year at the same venue.

I wonder was it there? I wonder was it at a matinée of *The Chasm*? I wonder was it in the Wee Hall, the Big Hall, or just out walking the streets? I wonder who made the first move and what exactly was said? I wonder a little unkindly did it help that there were fewer young men around that December? But wherever it was, whoever it was, and why ever it was right then, Jack and Kate finally met, or having met long since finally found themselves becoming more than friends: much, much more.

It was wartime, the silent era: I can't vouch for fireworks, but I like to think of the two of them quietly glowing through those short winter days and dark winter nights, and not with scarlet fever.

The only pity is that the festive season, like the famous frontline truce it inspired, had to end.

Fa-la-la-la-la-

la-la-, la-

la.

1915

Nineteen fifteen was the year of the unimaginable. The war that was supposed to have been over by Christmas carried on, if anything increased in ferocity and technological ingenuity. In January Germany launched the first air raids against civilian targets when a zeppelin dropped bombs on Yarmouth and King's Lynn, killing twenty people. (A twin-towers moment, surely, that: a shift in the global paradigm. Soon nowhere could be thought of as totally safe in wartime.) The East End of London was bombed on 31st May. By the end of the year casualties on home soil were running into the hundreds. At sea, submarine warfare came of dubious age with the sinking of the *Lusitania* off the coast of Kinsale and the loss of twelve hundred lives. Poison gas was used for the first time at the Second Battle of Ypres in April, and thereafter used and used and used again. (Twelve Lisburn men were to die in a gas attack in Belgium in September 1916.) Also bowing in, a week before the air raid on London, was the charge of 'crime against humanity', levelled by the Allied governments at Turkey over the massacres of Armenian Christians. From Loos in the west to Gallipoli in the east, meantime, men continued to be cut down in stupefyingly large numbers. No one pretended any more that an end was in sight.

One effect of this was to push up industrial demand and – night to its day – industrial wages. Ulster, for this war at least beyond the reach of the air-raiders, was especially well placed to benefit.* All of which might have had a bearing on Jack's decision in May 1915 to quit William J. Gillespie's, where he had now completed his apprenticeship, for a job at the Glenmore Bleach Works. Family tradition has it that he left in a dispute over money, a pay rise that never materialised. There is not the least hint of bad feeling, however, in the letter of recommendation with which William J. Gillespie sent him on his way: 'honest and obliging . . . trustworthy in whatever position in life he may be called on to fill'. True, he is leaving 'of his own accord', with – the letter is quick to add – 'all wages paid'. Perhaps those wages were just not on a par with the wartime linen trade. Perhaps not enough people were answering the patriotic call of Beckett Bros. and spending their increased wages on fancy goods and home furnishings, although I suppose they might have been

* Bardon, *Belfast*, p. 183, although the author does go on to say that wartime inflation meant that workers ended up having to work 'extremely long' overtime hours to maintain their standard of living. Food prices remained high despite attempts to ease the fear of shortages. The Province of Quebec, for instance, dispatched 46,000 eighty-pound cheeses to the United Kingdom, of which 1,316 were sent to Ireland. Of these, two – 160 pounds of cheese – were delivered to Lisburn, where, after they had been cut by the Lisburn Co-operative Society ('than whom there is no more generous concern'), their distribution was entrusted to Harold Barbour, younger brother of Sir Milne and chairman of the Lisburn Urban and Dunmurry Relief (Sub) Committee (*Lisburn Standard*, 15th January 1915). Somewhere in this equation might lie the answer to the question of where charity ends and cheeseparing begins.

Fancy Goods Warehouse 21 Bow Street.
Furniture Store and Manufactory 28 Bow Street.

CENTRAL FURNITURE STORES,

LISBURN May 1915

Glass, China, Delf, Stationery,
General Fancy Goods,
and Lamps of every description.

Shades and all Fittings.

Old Hair Mattresses Cleaned
and Remade.

Furniture Manufacturer,
Upholsterer,
and French Polisher.

Pure American Burning Oil
a Speciality.

THE ONLY
COMPLETE
HOUSE FURNISHER
IN LISBURN

ONLY
FIRST-CLASS WORKMEN
EMPLOYED.

To

MEMO. from
WILLIAM J. GILLESPIE,
House Furnishing Ironmonger and Hardware Merchant.

This is to Certify that the bearer John Patterson has completed his Apprenticeship In my employment during which time I always found him Sober, Honest and Obliging He now leaves of his own accord all wages being paid. I have no doubt he will prove himself trustworthy in whatever or whatever position in life he may be Called upon to fill He Carries with him my best wishes for his future success

Signed
Wm John Gillespie

spending so much in Beckett's that there was not enough left to go round the other shops on Bow Street.

All the same it does seem impetuous for a fully apprenticed young man to quit his trade in favour of millwork, and unskilled millwork at that.

I think of a conversation I once had with my cousin Ella.

Her mother, my Aunt Eileen, had a fiery temper: 'the red hair,' Ella said, 'like her own father's.'

Fiery? A man whose sternest rebuke when his children misbehaved was to place one forefinger on his lips and point with the other to the stairs up to their room? Still, that was after Jack had been delivered from his old self.* It is possible that a Jack none of us ever knew threw up the head as they say here (although even its red hair is hard for me to envisage) and walked out over a pay rise not granted. He was not yet averse to a bet. Perhaps, finally, he gambled his future earnings against a more immediate return, for a more pressing need. Kate, on the day he turned his back on shop work, was already four months' pregnant.

And then too his prospects had altered in one other significant way. The idea that he would apply the lessons learned at William J. Gillespie's to the Patterson family business depended, fairly obviously, on there still being a Patterson family business to apply them to. At some point in that year of 1915, however, the lease on 22 Smithfield passed, after almost four decades in Eleanor's name, to a man called James Hall. It is not clear what the catalyst was. Aggie and her husband Lawrence Hannon moved around this time to Kilwinning in Ayrshire to work in the munitions industry, but this may have been more a case of being pushed by circumstances than opting to jump. Eleanor, whether she was currently owning up to it or not, even to herself, was now in her early sixties. Her drinking – never less than steady – had

---

* It would make for a good reality TV show – or at least for one no worse than the rest – *Old Self and New Self Reunited*. Leave them for a weekend in a house with all Old's vices and only New's Big Book to swat them with. See what walked out the door on Monday morning. Or crawled.

for some time past been getting heavier. In all probability, and despite outward show, neither she nor the shop had recovered from her years of semi-detachment around the turn of the century. Number 9 Antrim Street, to which she now moved, was no more than a couple of hundred yards from 22 Smithfield, but in terms of status, and for a woman of her considerable pride (a woman who had once owned four acres just a little way up the road), it must have represented a pretty steep decline.

How her pride reacted to the news that her youngest son had got a Catholic mill girl pregnant is not hard to guess, even if much of the detail of what followed must for ever remain in the realm of speculation. The baby was born into the Ireland without records. For half a dozen years then there are few reliable co-ordinates, for my family any more than for other families. When all the machinery of state – or states – gets back into gear, in 1922, after the world war, the island against island war, the brother against brother war in the South and in the North the shooting-indiscriminately-at-the-the-other-sort war, Jack is living in 9 Antrim Street with his mother. Of Kate and her child there is still no trace, not in Antrim Street, not in 44 Chapel Hill. Actually all the Logues are gone now from Chapel Hill, but that is to get ahead of the story again.

As for what occurred in the spring and summer of 1915, Kate told it plainest to my own mother on a night when the two of them were left alone in Antrim Street shortly before Kate was admitted to hospital for the first and last time. Eleanor not only forbade Jack to marry her, she refused to let them have any kind of a life together, and never mind the baby – 'poor Eileen' – that Kate was carrying.

The revelation that there had been no marriage, but any amount of strife, was so out of the blue, so hard to reconcile with the 'naïve wee woman' sitting there making it, that my mother did not know what to think, much less what to say. She muddled through the minutes until the men returned (my father had been collecting Jack from a prayer meeting, she thinks, not exactly having to stick her neck out) and the subject was, unsurprisingly, not taken up again. A few weeks later Kate was dead. Looking back, my mother wondered if Kate had had an inkling that night that there would not be many more opportunities to – what? Confess? Or, in the strongest sense of the word, *complain*?

Looking back, she wished she had done more to encourage Kate to carry on talking: almost sixty years on, the pain of 1915 was still apparent.

Even allowing for her toleration of Lawrence Hannon, Eleanor's disapproval of Kate was hardly out of character. And Jack was different from Aggie, from all the other children. Not only was he the youngest, he was a Clements. The echo of her name in Eileen's – if echo is all it was – might have been intended to appeal to Eleanor's sense of fitness and due respect, but it cut no ice: the child would not be acknowledged.

'Eileen being born was like a curtain coming down,' was how my Uncle David summed it up. He and my Aunt Naomi had called at my parents' house one night with Edmund and his wife Isobel to have a look over the notes I had been making since our previous meeting almost a year before;* see if they could help turn a few of the question marks into full stops. A few of the other question marks at any rate . . . 'And it was successful,' David went on, 'because

* Giggs, Ronaldo (2), O'Shea, FYI.

here we are sitting all these years later trying to work out
what happened.'

The Cold War analogy of the curtain falling may have
been accidental, but it was apt. For if there was one word to
describe those previous generations of Pattersons, my father
and his brothers, Pattersons all, told me that evening, it was
cold, and pointed for evidence to the other Eileen, their
cousin, a couple of years my aunt's junior.

This younger Eileen was the daughter of Aggie and Lawrence Hannon. The couple had already had a child, Lyle, who
had died almost as soon as he was born and was buried in
Kilwinning, where they were still living. Perhaps with this
playing on her mind Aggie came home to Lisburn and her
mother during the later stages of her second pregnancy in the
opening months of 1918. Eileen was delivered without mishap
on 19th March. As soon as they were strong enough to travel,
Aggie returned with her daughter to Scotland, but two years
later she was back again, pregnant again. This time, however,
there was a double tragedy. Both Aggie and her baby – another
boy – died in the course of the labour in 9 Antrim Street.

Only three months earlier, Aggie's younger sister Emma
had fallen victim to the Spanish-flu pandemic that the Great
War had so neatly and devastatingly segued into. Although
settled in east Belfast among her husband's family, the
Moneypennys, Emma too had gone to her own mother's
house to be nursed, and to die. (She left behind two boys, the
eldest aged five.) It was a cruel mirror image of their quick-
succession weddings seven years before. I cannot begin to
think how much crueller it must have seemed to the mother
who was left to bury them: all three of her daughters gone to
the grave before her.

Lawrence Hannon survived his wife by less than a year, leaving Eileen, at not quite three, an orphan. At the time of her father's death she had been staying with Eleanor and Jack, but rather than be allowed to remain there she was now sent to live with her grandparents Hannon and their unmarried daughter, Lizzie, in the cottage in the townland of Derrymacash where Lawrence had grown up. If Antrim Street was a step down from Smithfield, the cottage, on the County Armagh shores of Lough Neagh, was, even in 1920, a step back in time from Antrim Street. One of Eileen's most vivid memories, from early on in this new life, is of her Granddad Hannon saying his prayers beneath a whin bush. She remembers, too, him making her a present of eels threaded on to a forked stick, and her fear of incurring Lizzie's wrath if she was caught bringing them into the house. (The fear got the better of her: she left the eels outside the door. The cat ate them.) Lizzie, indeed, seems to have been the dominant personality in the house. She was, says Eileen, with studied understatement, 'hard to live with'. And before Eileen was nine both her Granny and Granddad Hannon were dead too. Hard or not, there was only Lizzie to live with now.

'The Pattersons ostracised me,' she says bluntly.

She did go and stay once with her Uncle David and his wife Mary in Belfast, although she cried the whole time she was there, and she does have a few girlhood memories of her Uncle Fred. As for William, however . . . Many years later, now retired and on holiday in the south of England, Eileen was taken along to meet William and Dora's son Cecil, who was then living in Plymouth. The meeting it has to be said was something of a surprise to Eileen: she was not told until she was practically at the gate who it was she was going to see. It was a far greater surprise, though, to Cecil. He had never heard of her. William had practised what he preached. He had left the past well alone.

Cold.

Ask Eileen about Eleanor, on the other hand, and the reply is as spontaneous as it is surprising. 'She was never anything other than kind to me.'

She would come out to Derrymacash to visit from time to time in those final few years of her life, always with 'Uncle Jack', who drove the pony and trap they hired at the nearest train station, Lurgan, for the final leg of the journey. She was, even then, approaching seventy, and in spite of the years, the decades, of heavy drinking, a fine-looking woman: 'a good-sized woman', adds Eileen (who is five foot nothing) admiringly. Eleanor had made the gown Eileen was christened in.* She crocheted, besides, a purple coat and knit her a dark-red frock so distinctive that years afterwards, when it was being used as a floor cloth, a neighbour of Eileen and Lizzie's asked to borrow it so that she could copy the pattern.

Eileen was brought on visits to Antrim Street, too, occasionally. What is most telling of all about this period, though, is that she has no memory whatever of her cousin and namesake, Uncle Jack's own daughter, despite the fact that you could have covered the distance to Chapel Hill in not much more than a hop, a skip, and a couple of determined jumps.

The Logues, the Patterson boys are agreed, were warmer than the Pattersons. Yet even Daniel and Mary Jane had difficulty owning up to their illegitimate granddaughter.

---

* And not only Eileen: all of her Uncle Fred's children wore it, and their children. As recently as 1991 Emma Zoe, the youngest of his children's children's children, wore it. Swaddled in the knowledge of the 'townland of the flax pools'.

Kate on the night that she unburdened herself to my mother
said that when anyone called at the front door she would have
to take Eileen to the bottom of the garden, where she could
be seen by none but the fairies.* They must have spent a lot
of time out there in the winter of 1917. Two days after
Christmas that year Daniel died of bronchitis, to which mill
workers were of course particularly prone. And even at the
end of a third dispiriting year of a world war (Passchendaele,
with its half-million Allied casualties, and Cambrai in the
recent past) a death had to be waked in the proper way, no
end of people calling at the Logues' front door.

Daniel Logue was fifty-five on his death certificate, sixty-
one on his gravestone. The same gravestone records that he
was followed on his six-foot descent in April by William
Logue, his father, who had been born ninety-two years earlier
when George IV was on the throne and chumming around
with the third Marquis of Hertford, grandfather of Sir
Richard Wallace, Lisburn's favourite bastard child.

The nobility did illegitimacy differently, shame hardly at
all.

Eileen's first official sighting is not until 3rd June 1925,
when she turns up on the register of Lisburn Free National
School, or the Raggedy Bap as it was affectionately (if
obscurely) known, less than a month before the end of the
summer term, two-thirds of the way through her own tenth
year. In spite of her age she is admitted into the lowest class,

* My Uncle Edmund maintains that this too refers to Eleanor and the house
in Smithfield, whose garden he says stretched almost the length of Haslem's
Lane, with apple trees and plum trees at the far end. My mother, though, is
just as certain: Kate told her Chapel Hill; and anyway the electoral register
has James Hall in 22 Smithfield from 1915 on, the year of Eileen's birth.

Standard One – the clearest possible signal that this is not just a case of earlier records going missing, but of a child kept out of the system altogether. When the new school year starts in September she is there again, or at least is registered again. She only makes it to class seven days that autumn before on 24th October she is struck off the roll. Her entire schooling has amounted to four and a half teaching weeks.

You have to wonder, as you look through these records, at the strength of Eleanor's resolve. And you have to wonder too at Jack's utter lack of it. He wasn't a kid while all this was going on. But then, as my Uncle David declared, with unaccustomed vehemence, that night in my parents' house, this was a man who was still 'spouting tears' at the mere mention of his mother well into his sixties. It was very simple: Jack was a mummy's boy. When put to it he would sooner mollify her than defy her.

A Point of Principle

The two defining moments of the war years for Ireland north and south occurred within four months of one another in 1916. On the opening day of the Battle of the Somme, Saturday 1st July, the 36th Ulster Division, essentially eighteen battalions of the pre-war UVF, took just over five thousand casualties in twelve hours. Lisburn alone suffered the loss of 136 men, to go with the fourteen killed three days before the battle had even started when a German shell landed in the middle of their drill parade, although much good drilling did anyone once the signal had been given to go over the top. Together these deaths made up a sixth of the town's fatalities for the entire war. Thiepval Wood, on which much of that first day's fighting was centred, was commemorated in the name, if not the pronunciation, of the barracks (later army HQ) on the Magheralave Road.

Back in April, in Dublin, five hundred people – sixty per cent of them civilians – had been killed in the five days of the Easter Rising, which began on Monday 24th April with the seizure of the GPO on Sackville Street and Patrick Pearse's proclamation of an Irish Republic. With so many Irishmen

serving, and dying, overseas, however (Kate's brother-in-law
Tommy O'Neill was killed right in the middle of 'Easter
Week'), there was to begin with, even among Nationalists,
bewilderment and anger at the news. More than the proclamation, it was the British government's actions in the wake
of the Rising, in particular the execution of sixteen of its
leaders, that galvanised public opinion and guaranteed that
the political landscape was changed for ever. In the General
Election of December 1918 the Irish Parliamentary Party,
still wedded to the halfway house of Home Rule, was
annihilated by Sinn Fein, which promptly announced an
independent 'Dáil Éireann'. On the day in January 1919 that
this Dáil met for the first time a gang, eight or nine strong,
ambushed a consignment of explosives on its way to Solo-
headbeg Quarry in County Tipperary, killing the two-man
Royal Irish Constabulary (RIC) guard. Although the 'Volunteers' involved were not taking political direction when
they set their ambush their movement was gradually brought
under the control of the Dáil and the Irish Republican Army
was born.* The 'war' did not become general overnight, but
as the year progressed the city of Dublin and much of the
southernmost province of Munster were witness to many IRA
attacks and increasing numbers of reprisals by British troops
and members of the RIC.

Some of the worst fighting took place in County Cork,
birthplace of the IRA's director of intelligence, the Dáil's

---

* That, you would have thought, would have spelt an end, literally, for the
IRB, but the alphabetically challenged Brotherhood continued as an elite
cadre within the IRA for several more years. The Volunteers too persisted for
a time, at least in name. To this day it is the word the IRA prefers for its
members. Or to its last day it was the word it preferred, I should say. I really
should.

finance minister, Michael Collins. One of the few incidents outside of Dublin at the time of the Easter Rising was the siege in Castlelyons, near Fermoy, at the home of the strongly republican Kent family. Of four brothers in the house when the police raided, one, Richard, was fatally wounded – along with an RIC head constable – and a second, Thomas, was shot afterwards by firing squad. (Cork's Glanmire Road station was renamed Kent station on the fiftieth anniversary of the Rising, although only, somewhat meanly, after Thomas.) The county had as a result acquired, or appropriated to itself, the tag 'Rebel Cork'. All of which, for the time being at any rate, must have made it seem more than just a few hundred imperial miles from the other end of the island.

Ulster in the immediate post-war period was relatively quiet. In Belfast there was even the novelty of people taking to the streets for reasons that had nothing to do with sectarian politics, when, at the beginning of 1919, forty thousand engineering workers came out on strike in favour of a forty-four-hour week.

They lost, mind you, but all the same . . .

Then in Cork on the night of Friday 19th March 1920 the IRA shot dead an off-duty policeman, Constable Joseph Murtagh, on Pope's Quay, just across the River Lee from Cork Opera House. Although there had been many attacks in the county (on the night he died Murtagh was on his way home from a murdered colleague's funeral) this was the first fatal shooting of an RIC man in the city itself. A couple of hours later a group of anywhere between twenty and thirty men, at least some in civilian dress, others with their faces blackened, was seen on King Street, on the same side of the river, apparently having just left the RIC station. The men carried on – 'marching', according to eyewitnesses – up the steep Patrick's Hill and then on to Watercourse Road by way of Hardwick Street.

At the top of Watercourse Road, where it joined Thomas Davis Street (named for the leader of the 1848 Young Ireland rebellion and author of the anthem 'A Nation Once Again'), stood the house of Tomás MacCurtain, Sinn Fein Lord Mayor of Cork. MacCurtain was also the commanding officer of the IRA in the city (you have to hand it to Sinn Fein that so many of its members over the years were prepared to hold down two such demanding jobs) and so might have been suspected of having – expected to have, even – some knowledge of the murder of Joseph Murtagh. MacCurtain had, however, as soon as the news reached him, publicly commiserated with the dead policeman's family and was believed to be increasingly exasperated by the excesses of some of his own volunteers.* Besides, a warrant for his arrest had already been issued on the afternoon of the 19th March, which detracts further from the theory that what happened now in the early hours of the twentieth was a simple reprisal for the previous evening's murder.

What happened was that Tomás MacCurtain's wife Eilís heard a hammering at the front door. When she went to answer it half a dozen men burst past her into the hall. At least two of them made their way straight up the stairs and called on the Lord Mayor to come out of his bedroom. The instant he did he was shot in the chest at close range by a 'tall man in a light raincoat and blackened face'. Tomás MacCurtain died on the spot. He was two hours into his thirty-sixth birthday.

* Peter Hart, *The IRA and its Enemies: Violence and Community in Cork, 1916–1923* (Oxford University Press, 1998), p. 79. Even using the word 'news' here is to accept a lack of foreknowledge on the Lord Mayor's part.

In the wake of the shooting the Lord Lieutenant, Lord (formerly Field Marshall Sir John) French, let it be known that in his opinion Tomás MacCurtain had been murdered by his pals in the IRA, which was on a par with the suggestion, popular among the more squeamish republicans, that Constable Murtagh had been murdered by *his* pals in the RIC for refusing to go along with the plot to kill MacCurtain. Other rumours had Murtagh at the very heart of that plot, claiming that when he was shot he was found to have in his pocket 'material for blackening his face' – had already blackened his face, some said. The Roman Catholic Bishop of Cork was moved to issue a pastoral letter refuting the allegations: 'By these false theories the conscience of the people was drugged and their horror [of the murder] considerably lessened.'*

Just to complete the conspiracy circle MacCurtain is generally supposed to have been a member of the ambush party that narrowly failed in a bid to murder French as he was being driven through Phoenix Park in December 1919.

At the inquest into MacCurtain's death in April the fourteen-man jury not only took issue with the Lord Lieutenant's opinion, they cited him in their verdict as one of the guilty parties:

We find that the late alderman MacCurtain, Lord Mayor of Cork, died from shock and haemorrhage caused by bullet

* Reproduced on p. 222 of *The Burning of Cork* by Gerry White and Brendan O'Shea (Mercier, 2006). The earlier description of Tomás MacCurtain's killer is from *Rebel Cork's Fighting Story*, by Florence O'Donoghue et al., actually published in neighbouring – and rival – Kerry by Anvil Books, but still serving the Cork myth: 'It would not be within the competence of one man, not indeed of several men to set down in detail the story of Cork's contribution to the fight for freedom,' etc., etc.

wounds, and that he was wilfully murdered under circumstances of the most callous brutality, and that the murder was organised and carried out by the Royal Irish Constabulary, officially directed by the British Government, and we return a verdict of wilful murder against David Lloyd George, Prime Minister of England; Lord French, Lord Lieutenant of Ireland; Ian MacPherson, late Chief Secretary of Ireland; Acting Inspector-General Smith of the Royal Irish Constabulary; District Inspector Swanzy and some unknown members of the Royal Irish Constabulary. We strongly condemn the system at present in vogue of carrying out raids at unreasonable hours. [Is it me or does this, given the gravity of the other charges, seem a little quaint?] We tender to Mrs MacCurtain and family our sincerest sympathy. We extend to the citizens of Cork our sympathy in the loss they have sustained by the death of one so eminently capable of directing their civic administration.*

The police barracks on King Street was bombed and burned out by the IRA in July 1920. King Street itself, when Lord Lieutenants and Chief Secretaries of Ireland were no more, was renamed MacCurtain Street. It is where I was, or at least where I had ended up, on the night I met Ali, in the Síol Bhroin bar, across the street from the Garda Síochána station, because of course by then the Royal Irish Constabulary was

* Widely quoted. (I found it in O'Donoghue.) You could not argue with the wilful-murder verdict, although it should be pointed out that Sinn Fein had packed the jury with its supporters, just to be sure. It should also be pointed out that one of French's most trenchant critics was his sister, the romantic novelist, suffragette and eventual Sinn Fein member Charlotte Despard, who is buried in the republican plot in Dublin's Glasnevin Cemetery.

ancient history too.* One of the people who had helped make it so was Ali's great-aunt Rita, a member of – sorry, volunteer in – Cumann na mBan, the women's division of the IRA. Rita regularly carried messages, and more, into the men being held in Cork Prison. As cover she would sometimes take along her younger sister, Helena, known as Eily, and much, much later, to her grandchildren, as Gibby, who had explained to Ali when we were planning our wedding that my being Protestant could be fixed. Like I said, even in her middle eighties she gave the impression that she might have the connections.

Of all those accused in the inquest only one, District Inspector Swanzy, was actually resident in Cork at the time. He did not live to see the RIC's passing. In fact despite being moved out of the city within two months of Tomás Mac-Curtain's murder he did not live to see the end of the summer.

Oswald Ross Swanzy was two years older than Tomás MacCurtain and came from County Monaghan, although he had family ties further north. An ancestor, Henry Swansy [sic], had been born in the County Antrim parish of Blaris and christened in Lisburn Cathedral, between the fires, so to speak, in October 1666. He earned a commission in a local regiment raised to support the newly crowned King William III on his arrival in Ireland in 1690 and fought with him at the Battle of the Boyne before settling in Monaghan.

* The English translation of the bar's name is 'sad seed'; the anglicised version is Shelbourne, which the Síol Bhroin recently reverted to, citing on its website the 'about seven different pronunciations' of the name in the past. My own pronunciation varied according as I was going in or coming out.

Whether or not this had any bearing on the decision, Oswald Swanzy arrived to take charge of the police in Lisburn on 15th June 1920, moving into lodgings at 31 Railway Street with his mother and his sister Irene and attending Sunday service in the church where his great-great-great-great-grandfather was baptised. Lisburn, with its overwhelmingly Protestant population, must have seemed as safe a posting in Ireland as it was possible to contrive; Railway Street, with a police station at one end of it, beside the courthouse, as safe a street as any the town had to offer.

Back in Cork the IRA had already murdered two local RIC men – Sergeant Denis Garvey and Constable Daniel Harrington – in revenge for Tomás MacCurtain and was now stalking another senior officer with links to the North. Lieutenant-Colonel Gerald Brice Ferguson Smyth was born in the Punjab but grew up in Banbridge, County Down. He had lost his left arm at the Battle of Aisne in October 1914, when he also received an 'eight-inch by six-inch buttock wound', which by my reckoning (and buttocks) makes him an impressively built man.* Despite being eligible for a pension, he re-enlisted as soon as his convalescence was complete, and almost immediately was blown through a window in an accidental explosion at a bomb factory. He survived this as he survived another five serious combat wounds, including – God only knows how – a bullet through the neck at the Battle of Loos and a bullet to the chest in the

---

* At the time he was hit – by a high-explosive shell – he was rescuing a comrade lying wounded in the open. Kind of puts me and my buttocks joke in our place. See the not-at-all-partisan 'One-armed Irish Warrior of Dauntless Courage' by Paul McCandless at www.raymondscountydown-website.com.

German push of March 1918, and along the way picked up
the Distinguished Service Order and Bar, the French and
Belgian Croix de Guerre, the Mons Star, and a total of four
mentions in dispatches, although after all that you would
have thought he might have qualified for a dispatch bag with
his own name on it.

In June 1920 he was appointed Divisional Commander of
the RIC in Munster. Within weeks of his arrival he was at the
centre of a controversy in Listowel, County Kerry, where he
made a speech to the local RIC, which was interpreted by
some in his audience as a licence to shoot IRA volunteers on
sight. Constable Jeremiah Mee took off his cap, belt and
bayonet in protest, telling Smyth he could go to hell. When
the Lieutenant-Colonel ordered that Mee be arrested the
other constables refused so vehemently that Smyth and his
party were forced to withdraw from the barracks. This
'mutiny', or the speech that gave rise to it, made Smyth
an even greater hate figure for the IRA in Cork.

He was known to drink with other high-ranking officers in
the Cork and County Club on South Mall, the city's main
financial district, surroundings in which he evidently considered himself to be at little risk. At ten-thirty on the night
of 17th July, however, a gang of five, possibly six, IRA men,
among them Sean Culhane, intelligence officer with B
Company, 1st Battalion, managed to gain access to the club.
They made their way to the ground-floor smoking room,
where they singled out Smyth at his table and, the story goes,
told him *he* was now in sight, so had better prepare himself,
before opening fire. One eyewitness account describes the
bullets 'riddling' Smyth's face, forehead and neck. Con Casey
in the book *Rebel Cork's Fighting Story* specifies 'two bullets in

the head, one through the heart and two [more] through the chest'. Yet even then Smyth contrived to get to his feet and stagger into the hall before finally – survivor of Aisne and Loos and all that other lead – dropping to the floor dead. He was thirty-four.

Newspapers the following day reported the turmoil on the street outside the club in the aftermath of the assassination with the military having to (opting to?) fire shots as their ambulance tried to get through. They carried interviews with Ned Fitzgerald, one of the Cork and County Club waiting staff, who spoke of his shock, on answering a knock on the door, at finding himself confronted by the killers. In fact Ned Fitzgerald had been acting as an IRA spy for at least the past month; it was his tip-off that Smyth was in the club that night (Culhane's information was that he had gone away for the weekend) that brought the gunmen round knocking on the door. The shock would have been if they hadn't managed to get in.

An inquest the following week had to be abandoned. Not enough people in Cork could be found who were willing to sit on a jury.

Lieutenant-Colonel Smyth's funeral in Banbridge coincided with the return to work after the traditional 'Twelfth Fortnight' holiday in Ulster, where there were already signs things were on the slide. The IRA had been mounting sporadic attacks on the RIC in rural areas and as many as twenty people had been killed in repeated outbreaks of rioting in Derry. In his speech to Orangemen at Finaghy Field on 12th July, meanwhile, Sir Edward Carson had warned the government in London (that would be the same London government of which he had so recently been a part) that if need be Unionists would take matters into their own hands.*

That first Monday after the holidays, Nationalists – and socialists – were expelled from the shipyards and other Unionist-dominated places of work, although 'expelled' does not do justice to the violence of the forced departure. In some instances victims had to swim for their lives across Belfast's docks. 'A general hunt for Catholics' was the police's verdict, quoted by Henry McDonald in an article in the *Observer* in March 2000, marking the end of shipbuilding in Belfast.† Thirteen people died in three days and nights of rioting in the east of the city. Ominously there was rioting too, after the funeral, in Banbridge itself, where one person was killed and Catholic workers were again driven out of the factories and mills, only being allowed to return when (as in Belfast) they had signed a declaration that they were not members of Sinn Fein.

For the rest of the summer things remained calm, if tense; you wouldn't have had to be a genius to predict that very little was needed to spark even more savage sectarian violence.

It is rare that you would get through an entire book on Michael Collins without the 'g' word being invoked, so it would seem fair to assume that when he decided in the wake

* His words in fact could have been spoken by any Unionist leader any time in the next eighty-six years . . . eighty-six years, two months and a day, to be precise (see footnote p. 22): 'We in Ulster will tolerate no Sinn Fein – no Sinn Fein organisation, no Sinn Fein methods.' (Bardon, p. 190.)

† At least I *think* it has ended. Harland and Wolff remains, its website describing the company as 'a technically-led project management organisa- tion which is structured and organised to maximise opportunities in its chosen market sectors'. Does that say ships to you?

of the Smyth riots to pursue District Inspector Oswald
Swanzy he had taken into account the likely cost of a
successful mission and had judged that militarily, politically,
morally, it was worth paying.

> As I was in command, I decided to collect my evidence and
> play them at their own game. This was the start of the vicious
> circle – the murder race. I intercepted all the correspondence.
> Inspector Swanzy put Lord Mayor MacCurtain away, so I got
> Swanzy and all his associates wiped out, one by one, in all
> parts of Ireland to which the murderers had been secretly
> dispersed. What else could I do?*

I don't know what bothers me most, that final question, or
the sporting metaphors leading up to it. As for the latter,
there is a curious correspondence between Collins's words
here and a statement by the late David Ervine, leader of the
Progressive Unionist Party and sometime senior member of
the modern version of the UVF, to the effect that the Dublin
and Monaghan bombings of May 1974 (thirty-three dead)
were loyalism's way of 'returning the [IRA's] serve'. As for
the former, I am reminded of an article I tore out of the

---

* Another quotation from a book quoting a book. The quoter is Francis
Costello in *The Irish Revolution and its Aftermath, 1916–1923* (Irish Academic
Press, 2002), pp. 70–1; the quoted, Frank Crozier in *Ireland for Ever* (Cape,
1932), p. 218. Collins, by the way, is using what might be called the
'republican I' when he refers to the interception of correspondence. The main
interceptor was Matt McCarthy, an RIC sergeant and Collins's own cousin.
(It is worth remembering that the RIC at the time was almost seventy per
cent Catholic.) Billy Brown of the Northern Ireland Retired Police Officers
Association tells me McCarthy was stationed at Chichester Street in Belfast
in August 1920.

New Statesman and stuck on the wall above my desk while living in the flat on Bachelors Walk, trying to write my novel: a transcript of the commencement speech given by E. L. Doctorow at Brandeis University, near Boston, in October 1989.

'The philosophical conservative,' Doctorow told the students, and I highlighted it on the page ('A Gangsterdom of the Spirit', the article was called; I highlighted that too), 'the philosophical conservative is someone willing to pay the price of other people's suffering for his principles.'

Sean Culhane, the IRA intelligence officer who had taken part in the murder of Lieutenant-Colonel Smyth, was sent north in the third week of August 1920, armed, according to Irish republican folklore, with Tomás MacCurtain's own revolver. On arrival he made contact with Joe McKelvey and Roger McCorley of the IRA's Belfast Brigade. McKelvey, originally from County Tyrone, was one of the leading IRA figures in Ulster. An accountant by profession he had been a victim of the July expulsions, forced out of Mackie's engineering works on the Springfield Road. (As a barometer of Protestant–Catholic relations, Mackie's, midway between the Shankill Road and the Falls, was to west Belfast what the shipyard was to the east.) He had only been working in the factory a matter of months, having previously been employed in the city's tax office, which he himself had helped burn down in April.

McCorley had already carried out reconnaissance in Lisburn, making so bold as to exchange pleasantries with Oswald Swanzy on one occasion as he strolled in Castle Gardens. There is even a suggestion that he had had the policeman tailed on his summer holiday to the Isle of Man.*

On Sunday morning, 22nd August, a taxi left the Belfast Motor Cab and Engineering Company in the city's Upper Library Street. At the wheel was twenty-five-year-old Sean Leonard from Tubbercurry, County Sligo, who had been chauffeuring for the company (they wore hats in those days) for a year. He had a booking for a quarter to twelve at the Great Northern Railway station in the city centre. The fare, a Mr Brady, had apparently expressed an interest when he phoned in taking a run along the County Down coast. 'Mr Brady' was, in fact, McKelvey, Culhane and another Cork man, Dick Murphy.† The taxi headed not for the coast, but inland, to Lisburn, where it parked on Castle Street, outside the Municipal Technical College. (Hello, Henry Munro and the Lisburn Loyal Infantry.) McCorley and a colleague named Tom Fox were already in the town for a final scout.

Summer Sundays were ever days for strolling and chatting

* The account that follows draws on a number of sources: Alan F. Parkinson, *Belfast's Unholy War* (Four Courts Press, 2004); Robert Lynch, *The Northern IRA and the Early Years of Partition* (Irish Academic Press, 2004); *The Burning of Cork*, previously mentioned, by Gerry White and Brendan O'Shea; *Police Casualties in Ireland, 1919–1922*, by Richard Abbott (Mercier Press, 2000); and on contemporary newspaper reports. There are inevitably contradictions between them, sometimes within them. This is my best guess at the sequence of events.

† White and O'Shea have several other members of the Cork Brigade present: Leo Ahern, Jack Coady and Christy McSwiney; although even by the standards of Belfast taxis this is maybe pushing it a bit. *Was* pushing it a bit: Lynch says that an attempt to kill Swanzy two weeks before was called off when the overloaded car broke down; hence the slimmed-down gang of 22nd August. White and O'Shea incidentally also name McSwiney as one of the gunmen who murdered Constable Joseph Murtagh back in March.

to friends. No one paid much attention to Culhane and Murphy as they walked the hundred or so yards from the car to the corner of Castle Street and Railway Street, where they joined McCorley and Fox, already waiting outside Boyd's pharmacy, facing the Northern Bank and across the road from the side gate to Lisburn Cathedral. A couple of minutes after one o'clock the congregation began to emerge from this and the main gate on Cross Row. Swanzy, who had called into the RIC barracks at the other end of Railway Street before going to morning service, left the church in the company of Mr Fred Ewart and his son Major Gerald Ewart. (The major's brother, Captain Cecil Ewart, had been among the dead at Thiepval Wood.) Culhane would presumably have recognised Swanzy straight away, even without McCorley's assistance. Whether Swanzy would have been able to place the Cork man's face so unexpectedly out of context will never be known. Before he even had time to turn, the four IRA men, 'respectably dressed', according to eyewitnesses, made a sudden dash across the street and opened fire – Culhane of course with Tomás MacCurtain's revolver – from a distance of about six yards, hitting Swanzy below the right ear. After pushing the Ewarts out of the way the gunmen fired again and again, putting a total of five bullets into the District Inspector's head and body as he lay on the street. Then they beat a retreat – 'legged it as fast as they could run', one witness said – with McCorley turning and crouching now and then to provide covering fire.

Incredibly, at least to me (loud bangs frighten me, I bleed easily), a number of people kept up the pursuit, all the way back to the taxi. Captain Alex Woods, commandant of the UVF in the town (the Royal Irish Rifles having clearly morphed back after the Armistice) was leaving the cathedral a short distance behind Swanzy. He went after the gang with his blackthorn stick until a bullet broke it clean in two. Another bullet passed through the dress of a Miss McCreight, grazing her side; another broke the plate-glass window of the Co-op boot shop, opposite the cathedral's side gate.

In his haste to get away, Leonard started the taxi before the other four were all on board. McCorley had to dive inside, whereupon his gun went off a final time, the bullet piercing the floor and embedding itself in the road. The taxi sped off along Seymour Street, where it was the 'white, staring faces of the occupants' that struck those who saw it pass, then on to the Belsize Road, from where it was able to take one of the numerous C roads into the countryside and, despite being chased by requisitioned cars, make good its escape.

And that was that. Tomás MacCurtain – the city of Cork – was avenged, Michael Collins satisfied: he had done the only thing he could see to do. Sean Culhane formally handed over MacCurtain's revolver to Collins that night, amid much backslapping, in a hotel on Parnell Square, not far from Amiens Street (now Connolly) station. He had been led to believe that Collins would one day return it to him as a keepsake. He never did. Two years later, to the very day (two years and, fatally, one divisive treaty with the British later), Collins himself was shot dead by Anti-Treaty republicans in an ambush at Béal na mBláth in his 'rebel' home county.*

---

* The Anti-Treaty forces continued to call themselves the IRA, although their opponents preferred the term 'Irregulars'. The Pro-Treaty forces became the National Army. Both sides in Irish were Óglaigh na hÉireann. It would take, oh, let's see, the better part of a hundred years for them to solve the problem of which had greater claim to legitimacy. (You have solvd it now, lads, haven't you?)

Although he took no part in the ambush, Sean Culhane was one of the Anti-Treaty brigade staff in the area at the time. Three months later again, Joe McKelvey was summarily executed in Dublin in retaliation for the shooting of one of Collins's fellow 'Free State' Dáil members. In that time more than four hundred people had been killed in Belfast alone, among them the uncle of *Observer* columnist Henry McDonald, a Catholic who was dragged off a tram by loyalists at Bridge End, close to the shipyards, and beaten to death.

Nothing quite so appalling ever happened in Lisburn, but, although a handful of its citizens had displayed considerable courage in pursuing Oswald Swanzy's killers on the August morning he was shot, neither could the town claim to have covered itself in glory in those years – in those next few hours particularly. Sackcloth would be more appropriate. Ashes.

'Lisburn's Red Sunday'*

To anyone who lived through the final third of the last century in Northern Ireland, much about the planning and execution of Oswald Swanzy's murder will sound horribly familiar. For all that the act itself may be quickly accomplished, politically motivated murder is a labour-intensive affair. One Saturday in April 1991, my second year in Lisburn, Ernest McCrum, a police sergeant nearing retirement, was working in his wife's antiques shop round the corner from Bachelors Walk, at the lower end of Antrim Street, when gunmen entered and shot him dead. No one else was in the shop at the time, so there is no way of knowing how many gunmen all told, or what precisely transpired in the moments before the fatal shots were fired, although it is clear that Sergeant McCrum, who had been on police sick leave for several weeks, did not stand a chance. His personal-protection firearm was still in its holster when his body was found. His killers locked the door behind them (so they stayed long enough to locate the keys, or, worse, asked for

* Front-page headline of the *Belfast Telegraph*, 23rd August 1920.

them before shooting), presumably to prevent the alarm being raised before they were clear of the town. The first anyone was aware of the murder was when the IRA volunteer tasked with making this sort of call phoned a local radio station. The car used in the killing was found abandoned in west Belfast, from where it had earlier been hijacked by still another IRA team. Police eventually uncovered the murder weapon in the search of a house whose occupants in all likelihood had no idea where the gun had been between its being picked up and returned to them for hiding.*

I had been in Belfast that afternoon, having my photograph taken for the *Daily Telegraph*, along with other young movers and shakers, in Nick's Warehouse, a wine-bar then newly opened on Hill Street – the first in the city, just as the *Telegraph*'s was the first of the Belfast-baby-steps-into-the-light type features I can remember reading. The features would recur with increasing frequency over the next decade and a half, whenever a new political deal was in the offing, or a building fronted entirely by glass (glass! Belfast!) was unveiled. I know. I wrote quite a few of them myself.

I arrived back in Lisburn a couple of hours after the killing to find Bachelors Walk solid with traffic being diverted away from Antrim Street. Ernest McCrum's body still lay in the shop exactly as it had been found to allow forensics officers time to complete their examination, but the other shops and businesses I passed on the way to my flat remained open. That is the chief difference between the earlier killing and the later

* David McKittrick, Seamus Kelters, Brian Feeney and Chris Thornton, *Lost Lives* (Mainstream, 1999). The book contains 3,636 such descriptions, from John Patrick Scullion's murder in Clonard, west Belfast, on 11th June 1966, to Charles Bennett's thirty-three years later, half a mile further up the Falls Road.

one: the response of the police and the public at large. By 1991
Northern Ireland had, per capita, the biggest police force in the
western world (not quite the boast that biggest shipyard once
was), with a seven-hundred-strong CID ready to swing into
full investigative mode at a moment's notice. Assuming, that
is, there were no Special Branch informers to protect. For
everyone else, murder was a cause for pause, for rethinking the
route home, scarcely any more a reason even to stop shopping.

On the day Oswald Swanzy was murdered there were no
more than six or seven police officers in all of Lisburn. The
townspeople had never known the like of it for horror.

In 31 Railway Street Oswald Swanzy's sister Irene had
heard the shots and at once started running in the direction
from which they had come. She arrived while Dr George St
George, surgeon at the County Antrim Infirmary on Seymour
Street, was ministering to her dying brother, although some
reports have him dead almost as soon as he hit the ground.
Irene was able to cradle his head for a few moments before the
body was lifted into the Northern Bank and then, a short
time later, carried on a stretcher back to the Swanzy house,
followed by a 'deeply sympathetic crowd'. Within half an
hour the numbers on Railway Street – a crime scene, don't
forget – had swollen to two thousand and the mood had
changed from sympathy to rage. A rumour spread that some
of the IRA gang were hiding in the cathedral graveyard,
which drew the crowd out of Railway Street, on to Cross Row
(today's Market Square East), whose yard walls backed right
on to the cathedral grounds. Here, the rumour mutated, shots
had been fired from the upstairs of Mrs Gilmore's confectionery shop. The owner's son was said to be a 'Sinn Feiner' –
a term that, even more than in later decades, was used as a

synonym for member of the IRA. A section of the crowd prevailed upon the few police officers present to search the premises, but when the search yielded neither gunman nor son, the officers departed. Into the vacuum they left poured the people who had been waiting outside. They rampaged through the shop and the living quarters above, throwing furniture into the street where it was broken up and burned.

This set the tone for all that was to follow.

Just around the corner from Cross Row, on Bridge Street, was McKeever's bar, whose owner, Peter McKeever, had only recently moved back to Ireland from Canada and was, more to the point, like Mrs Gilmore, a Catholic. This bar too was now broken into and in the course of its being looted the cry went up again, from inside the bar, that shots had been fired – that someone had been wounded. And indeed the cry this time had substance, except the victim of the shooting was Peter McKeever himself, hit in the chest as he struggled with one of the looters. The looting went on around him. When at length an ambulance arrived from the County Infirmary it was met with shouts of 'Colonel Smyth did not get an ambulance and he will not', which was very grammatically correct of whoever was doing the shouting. The ambulance was then *shoved* down Bridge Street towards the River Lagan.*

Peter McKeever was shot at half past two, but it was to be another three hours before friends could reach him to

---

* Shoving vehicles down Bridge Street had a bit of a pedigree. Back in the early 1890s a circus that had been too slow setting up was literally run out of town by impatient punters (shunters?) who dragged several wagons – one inlaid with mirrors – from Smithfield to the top of Bridge Street, from where they launched them into the Lagan. (*Lisburn Standard*, 10th October 1891.) You wouldn't condone it, but still – a freewheeling wagon with mirrors! – you would pay good money to see it.

smuggle him out of the bar, which also backed on to the cathedral grounds. The friends carried him in a quilt through the gravestones towards Seymour Street and the hospital.

A detachment of the Norfolk Regiment had arrived in the town in the meantime and the cathedral bell had been rung, it seems to rally the 'Volunteers' (volunteers of the other persuasion, that is) to help maintain order. None answered its summons, strongly suggesting, if the shooting of Peter McKeever was not suggestion enough, that some at least of those being summoned were already involved in the disorder on the streets. Not long afterwards an attempt was made to set light to one of the Norfolks' vehicles parked on Cross Row.

Having got a taste for the task with McKeever's (more potent than ransacking a sweetie shop) the looters were now moving down through the town, seeking out bars with Catholic owners. McClarnon's, McKenny's, Neeson's and Connolly's 'Vine Hotel' were all raided and burned. (You don't get to be a hotel-free city without someone putting in the effort.) At the bottom of Market Street one group peeled away, left, into Linenhall Street and set fire to the 'Wee Hall', home of the Hibernians and venue for so many Saturday-night dances.*

In Haslem's Lane William Shaw, a Sinn Fein councillor, was dragged out of his house and beaten up, although he managed somehow to make his way on foot through the mayhem to the County Infirmary, where he was treated by the same Dr St George who had earlier tried to resuscitate

---

* These were tough, tough times for the Hibernians. The IRA was also burning their halls, due to the order's close identification with the Nationalist Party, rival to Sinn Fein for the Catholic vote.

Oswald Swanzy. The crowd meanwhile were making a
bonfire of William Shaw's belongings in the middle of
Haslem's Lane. They did the same, a short time later, outside
the home of James Stronge, another Sinn Fein member, on
Bachelors Walk.*

Further up Bachelors Walk, at its junction with Railway
Street, the Railway and Commerical Hotel – the future
Robin's Nest – had been set about and most of its
ground-floor windows smashed.† Just when it seemed an
all-out assault was imminent, acting District Inspector
Moore of the RIC, who had only just arrived from Larne
to take charge of the police operation, appeared at an upstairs
window, urging calm. (I see that window seventy years later
with posters advertising the reading I have organised: *Tonight! Michael Longley, Desmond Hogan, Robert McLiam Wilson.
Bar 8 till Late* . . .) No one, Moore called down to the street,
regretted the death of his dear friend District Inspector

* On Tuesday morning a car full of men arrived at the County Infirmary,
demanding to be allowed to see Councillor Shaw. Dr St George told them
that the patient was in no fit state to be released, but Shaw insisted on
discharging himself. He left the hospital between two of the men, a
waterproof sheet over his head, and was driven off in the direction of
Belfast. It seems certain the IRA carried out the rescue, although Dr St
George would later tell a court that Shaw was not under any sort of threat
and that in any case he, St George, would have laid down his life before
allowing any patient in the infirmary to suffer injury. At roughly the same
time, one of the few local people arrested in connection with the rioting was
being sprung by a crowd, which threatened, all too plausibly, to burn down
the RIC station on Barrack Street.
† Charles Brett singled it out for praise: 'a very fine solid frilly building'. (A
very Brettian description.) 'On each front, good lettering, fluted Doric
columns; a pleasant iron balcony joining charming two-light window oriels
(at first-floor level); much good stucco ornament.' It was painted grey when I
lived across the road from it. Top to bottom, grey.

Swanzy more than himself, but all this destruction would not bring back the life that had been taken.

Jack had always told my father that he saw the mob – for it was unquestionably a mob by now – outside the Railway Hotel that day. He told him that the ringleader was John Wylie. The same John Wylie whose name appears (I look at it one more time to be certain) on the third page of Jack's Faith Mission diary, and who was one of the repertory company of names – Nell Connor, Minnie Connor, Cecil and Billy Parkinson – on which the conversations that went on above my head in 9 Antrim Street seemed always to draw. I met him myself when I was a child, as I met all of that company. Dapper, is about as much as my memory offers up. Not tall.

He was standing on a crate outside the Railway Hotel, Jack told my father, the better to be heard.

LISBURN'S RED SUNDAY.

THE SLAYING OF MR. SWANZY

FULL STORY OF GRIM DEED.

ASSASSINS' DARING GET-AWAY.

WILD SCENE OF RIOT FOLLOWS.

On Sunday at midday the streets of Lisburn in Bow Street was ablaze. The latter burn never presented a quieter appearance. At one o'clock, the church services having concluded, the worshippers were passing homeward, Railway Street corner being a converging point for the congregations from the Cathedral, Christ Church, Market Square,

premises are adjacent to Messrs. Bucksst's large drapery establishment, and the firemen transferred their attentions to save this building.

In Lisnahall Street the Hibernian Hall was gutted, and in Smithfield the licensed premises of J. M'Larnon and J. Neeson.

I read the newspaper reports from the day after Oswald Swanzy's murder and I wonder if John Wylie's is the voice of the 'spokesman' who shouted back at DI Moore that since the government clearly could not deal with these murderers the loyal people of Lisburn would have to do it themselves. They would 'continue the destruction until sympathisers of the murderers were ordered from the town'. (Again, you have to admire the command of grammar in the – by now pretty extreme – heat of the moment.) 'The people of Lisburn believed in a life for a life, and if they could not get the Sinn Feiners to fight them in the open, then the Unionists were determined that the cowards would be cleared out of their midst.'

What this meant in practice was an intensification of the afternoon's rampage. The Norfolk Regiment was guarding the approaches to the Sacred Heart of Mary Convent on Castle Street and to St Patrick's Church – to the bulk of the town's Catholic population – on Chapel Hill. In between these two poles, and with the exception of the Railway Hotel, which after the exchange just noted was spared, the town was effectively unprotected. (Shades here of August 1969 when the first troops into Belfast stood, stoic beneath their Second World War tin hats, in entirely the wrong place, while a quarter of a mile away all hell was breaking loose.) In the hours that followed, the mob looted and burned butchers, drapers, hardware stores, cycle works, grocer shops, shoe shops, delph shops and bar after bar after bar.

Adair's paint shop was ransacked, putting yet more fuel in the hands of the arsonists. You can't beat varnish for a nice finish to a building.

Jefferson's timber yard went up, so did Burns' fruit and veg.

Poor Burns. Poor Lisburn and its fatal attraction to flames.

Sean Culhane saw the fires light up the evening sky as he travelled south on the train from Belfast to Dublin, still carrying the murder weapon – the totem – with which to present Michael Collins.

He had opted for a first-class compartment, reasoning, correctly, that he would attract less attention there.*

When the pall-bearers carrying Oswald Swanzy's coffin emerged from 31 Railway Street the next morning to walk the short distance to the station for the ten o'clock Dublin train – Mount Jerome Cemetery at the journey's end – there were still people on the streets from the night before: from the lunchtime before, many of them. Much of Bow Street and Market Square was smouldering. Some of the shops that had come through the night unscathed were flying Union Jacks to discourage any future attempts on them. Few of them were open.

At midday Swanzy's inquest got underway in the court-house. (No trouble, this time, finding a jury.) In the course of the proceedings a lawyer levelled accusations of complicity in the murder at local Catholics and at the people of Cork for 'fabricating and broadcasting stories'. Meanwhile a hundred or more men, women and children were converging on Henry Dornan's butcher shop on Market Square, where the single policeman on duty, Sergeant Edgar, was unable to prevent

---

* Lynch, p. 35. I have no way of corroborating it, but I would bet my astronomical publisher's advance that the IRA was still exploiting this 'class' bias in the 1980s, when I was standing in my jeans and leather jacket trying to convince Special Branch men at Heathrow (and Gatwick and Birmingham and Manchester) that the specimen signature I had just provided them with did match the one on my student card, while the – ahem – businessmen slipped past unchallenged.

another fire being started. (Months later, in court, he would describe the majority of those present as 'essentially decent sorts made insensible by drink'.) And so it began again. More butchers, more grocers, more bars and some of yesterday's targets revisited. A boot factory in Graham Gardens looted on Sunday was now burned out completely. Somewhere in the middle of all this the Comrades of the Great War building on Bow Street caught fire.

During the afternoon the Urban Council met in emergency session – with apologies, I am assuming, from its Sinn Fein members – and decided to cut off the gas supply in an attempt to starve the flames of fuel. Councillors also resolved to patrol the streets as a body that evening and enlist the help of 'respectable citizens' in persuading their less respectable brethren to return to their homes after dark.

Independently of this, Revd Canon Carmody, Dean of Christ Church, had called a meeting in the cathedral schoolroom earlier in the day of people willing to assist the police and army in restoring order. Attendance was small. Canon Carmody assured those who had turned up that they were not protecting Sinn Feiners, 'who were not there to defend', but the town itself. And anyway, many of the businesses that had been destroyed belonged to 'loyal, Protestant people', who were going to have to foot the bill in increased rates.

The dean had sought, and received, assurances from army commanders that there was to be no martial law in the town, no curfew, nothing more compelling in fact than a notice to quit the streets by eight o'clock. This notice having been given and ignored, Canon Carmody's citizens' patrols set out at half past eight. Among their number was the Revd Henry Swanzy, the dead policeman's cousin, who had travelled up from his parish in Newry. In Market Square he read an appeal for calm from the bereaved mother and sister, saying that Oswald would not willingly have hurt the smallest of God's creatures and was so utterly above feelings of revenge that it would have been a real grief to him that anyone should suffer pain or loss on his account.* This too was ignored. During the evening, indeed, someone started a fire in the newsagent's next to Canon Carmody's house on Castle Street and only the swift arrival of the army prevented the dean being added, however notionally, to the list of the homeless.

The local fire brigade by this stage was completely overwhelmed. (A photograph taken in the 1930s suggests a full complement for the town of only fourteen firemen.) Earlier in the day the Belfast Brigade had sent some of its units to assist, but it withdrew them again at seven o'clock after their hoses were repeatedly cut. The only check now on the arsonists was their own energy and ingenuity after more than thirty hours of destruction and, in a great many cases, continuous drinking.

On Cross Row, where it had all begun, Pelan's pawnshop was looted and burned (did the looters restrict themselves to taking what was already theirs?), so too was the ice-cream parlour belonging to Pietro Fusco, who lived above the shop with his wife Santina and their three young sons, Philip, Dominic and Giovanni. On Bridge Street McCourtney's confectionery and fancy bakery shop was wrecked and the contents of its living quarters dragged out on to the street, where children entertained themselves by 'playing' a piano with

---

* Well, they would say that, you might think, although in relation to Tomás MacCurtain at any rate, one of Cork's most prominent IRA figures, Captain Florence O'Donoghue, later expressed grave doubts about Swanzy's guilt (Hart, p. 79).

sticks. One 'nipper', according to the *Belfast Telegraph*, even weighed in with a sledgehammer. (Big nipper or small sledge?)

All of this, though, and despite the enthusiasm with which they went at it, was really just a diversion from what had been the target since the crowd marched out of Railway Street and on to Cross Row the previous afternoon: 'Sinn Feiners . . . sympathisers of the murderers', or, very simply, Catholics.

It was only a matter of time before the focus shifted on to Chapel Hill. And, let's face it, even doing some of the places twice, there was only so much of the rest of the town left to burn.

By early evening as many as a thousand people, a tenth of the total population, were massed before the army lines at the junction of Chapel Hill and Bow Street. Maybe some of them paused from their exertions to refresh themselves at the nearby Wallace Fountain, if not (more is the pity) to reflect on the spirit of the Commune that it commemorated: religion as a matter of individual conscience, anybody? On the contrary, the *Irish News* has the mob crying, as it had cried the day before outside the Railway Hotel, 'Give us the Scriptures – an eye for an eye and a tooth for a tooth!' Whether it was the blunt force of this theological argument, or the sheer weight of the numbers bearing down on them, or whether indeed there was an element of strategy involved, as the evening wore on the soldiers fell back to the chapel precinct and in effect wrote themselves out of the narrative of the next several hours. Almost at once the first fires broke out at the bottom of the hill. Looters targeted shops then, inevitably, bars: Lavery's, Quinn and Downey's, and – one of the worst fires of the night – Dan Mooney's 'Empire Hotel'. In the meantime, impatient perhaps for army tactics to manifest themselves, a section of the crowd had bypassed the street entirely and was making its way via the Fairy Mount to the parochial house off Longstone Street, a little above Chapel Hill.

Finding this 'most commodious' – evidently the 'luxury' of its day – 'and beautifully situated' house undefended they gutted it, destroying thousands of parish records in the process and leaving the walls daubed with slogans: 'No Pope or Papists Here', and 'New Orange Hall'.*

The parish priest had left some time during the afternoon, no doubt fearing just such an attack. He was not alone. Many other Catholics had already opted to take what they could carry and abandon their homes. It was still possible in the

* It occurs to me that this fire – Lisburn's own mini Four Courts – might have contributed to my Aunt Eileen's decade of invisibility, although I have also heard it suggested that the bulk of the records had been successfully removed to the safekeeping of St Malachy's College, Belfast. If they did go, they never came back. That's St Malachy's for you. Once they get hold of you you're theirs for life.

earlier part of the day for those who could afford it to leave town, unmolested, by taxi, even by train. Some headed to Belfast, some to the safer south.

Many more, though, stayed put, perhaps trusting that the army could – surely would – protect them, that the government would not permit such lawlessness to go unchallenged; perhaps not believing that people they met day to day, socialised with, did business with – people they had grown up with – could honestly mean to do them harm.

So when the troops withdrew to St Patrick's around half past eight on Monday night, allowing the mob free run of Chapel Hill, a significant number of the residents were still within doors. Patrick Magee, hiding in his cellar with a neighbour, John Hegarty, watched as his own furniture was trailed out on to the street and set alight. Three adjoining houses, almost directly facing the chapel, and on the Longstone Street side of Quinn and Downey's, were attacked at the same time. The *Lisburn Standard* published on Friday 27th August catalogues the consequences:

> **CHAPEL HILL.**
>
> **William Gilmore** (general dealer)—Looted.
>
> **Hugh M'Evoy** (tailor)—Burned out.
>
> **Mrs. Martin** (confectioner)—Burned out
>
> **Daniel Mooney** (publican)—Burned out.
>
> **Robert Bell** (private house)—Burned out.
>
> **Quinn & Downey** (publicans)—Burned out.
>
> **Henry Bradley** (private house)—Wrecked and looted).
>
> **Mrs. Moran** (private house)—Wrecked and looted.
>
> **Mrs. Logue** (private house)—Wrecked and looted.

I have not found a living soul who can tell me whether Mary Jane, Kate and Eileen were in the house when the wreckers and looters reached it, or, if they got out, when they did, and where they went to next, unless of course they took refuge at the bottom of that great big garden Kate always insisted that they had.

What is certain is that in the wake of the assault on Chapel Hill the majority of Catholics who remained in the town now fled. For most this meant a night in the open, in countryside on the edge of town. Not a few started to walk into the Glenavy Hills on the western outskirts and did not stop until they had reached Belfast, eight miles away on the other side. This 'tramp over the mountains' continued into Thursday when scores of refugees, some suffering from exposure, turned up at the doors of St Mary's Hall, looking for help from the relief committee set up after the disturbances in July. The hall was attached to the church that had opened with the support of the Protestant Volunteers at the end of the eighteenth century. In the spring of 1922 police raided the hall, uncovering bombs, bullets and a briefcase full of IRA documents in an office being used by the charitable St Vincent de Paul Society.*

In Lisburn that second morning after Red Sunday Catholics who had, despite everything, clocked in for work at Stewart's Flax Mill on Antrim Street were confronted by

---

* Details of this find might. read like something dreamed up on the paranoid fringes of Free Presbyterianism, but in fact are taken from Robert Lynch's very sober *Northern IRA* book. And, you have to say, what tubes the Northern IRA could be. St Vincent de Paul. A church hall. For fuck's sake.

Protestant colleagues demanding they sign a loyalty pledge: 'I hereby declare I am not a Sinn Feiner nor have any sympathy with Sinn Fein and do declare that I am loyal to king and country.' When the Catholic workers refused, to a woman and man (a woman and a man might have been about all there were), they were made to leave. The same thing happened at the Barbour Threads Mill in Hilden, where Kate had been working, not that I could see too many of her friends braving the streets that morning, even with their arms linked. Two young Catholic men who spoke to the *Irish News* on their arrival in Belfast late on Tuesday were adamant that all their co-religionists had been hounded out of the town, irrespective of age or circumstance. The paper called this 'wiping out' of the Catholic population a 'worse-than-German persecution . . . The Belgians were not treated so harshly and foully as the innocent Catholics of Lisburn'.

The *Lisburn Herald* accused the *Irish News* – or at least the 'nationalist press', which at that time in the North amounted to the same thing – of exaggerating the effects of the riots. Many of the town's Catholics were going about

their lives and businesses free from threat, it claimed, and might have pointed for proof to the nun snapped by a newspaper photographer walking through the mess of Bow Street, although from the way everyone else in the shot is mugging for the camera an elephant could have been walking down the street and not been noticed. No doubt the *Herald* would have questioned too the impartiality of the radical *Daily News* (founder and former editor Charles Dickens), which put the number expelled at 'about a thousand', and would not even have entertained the figure of thirteen hundred that appeared a decade and a half later in St Patrick's Church's own *Catholic Year Book and Blotter and Calendar*. (The town, the *Year Book* says, was 'practically deserted' by Catholics in the aftermath.) However, even so ardent a Unionist as Major Fred Crawford – old blood-for-ink himself – seemed awed by the extent of the devastation when he visited the town on Tuesday. He slipped over the Belgian border for his own analogy: like a bombarded town in France, he wrote in his diary, adding that in his estimation there were no more than four or five Catholic families left in all of Lisburn. Typically, though, his real concern was reserved for those 'hard cases' where the homes of Protestants living next to Catholics had caught fire.

'All this is done by Unionists as a protest against these cold-blooded murders,' he said, as though the hymn-sheet doing the rounds of Bachelors Walk and Chapel Hill had now been passed (only slightly singed) to him. 'The victims are Rebels and their Sympathisers.'*

It is easy, I know, to be dewy-eyed about your own family, but really you have to ask who in their right mind (I am obviously excluding Major Crawford himself here) could have felt threatened by a window, a wee fairy and a five-year-old girl.

My father, as in the dark about much of this as I was when I started, reminded me on several occasions that all of Kate's sisters and more than one of her brothers had married Protestants. Surely, whatever about Eleanor's antipathy to her, these broader-minded siblings would not have left Kate and her mother and Eileen to fend for themselves?

My own speculation on those two days of mayhem – for by Tuesday night the worst was over – would return invariably to Jack. The more I thought about him seeing John Wylie whipping up the mob out the front of the Railway Hotel, the more I worried that he might not have been the detached observer his account suggests. The town was in ferment that afternoon. It seems unlikely that he was simply out for a dander. And even if he were doing no more than trying to gauge the temperature (boiling, continuing to rise) would it not have been obvious to him, given what had happened in Banbridge and Belfast the previous month, how the hunt for 'Sinn Feiners' was bound to pan out? Did he turn around and pelt, as though his daughter's life depended on it, back down

---

* This from the second great Jonathan Bardon book of recent years: *A History of Ulster* (Blackstaff Press, 1992). Robert Lynch also quotes from the diary, but includes a passage in which Crawford visits the ruined parochial house and finds 'a small pair of manicure scissors' in the rubble. He kept them as a souvenir.

Bachelors Walk, left along Antrim Street, round the corner and up Chapel Hill, to tell Kate to grab Eileen and come with him? Or did he mentally stall, before he had even started, at the door of number 9 and the spectre of his mother's ire?

I thought too about the assertion that many were born again in the Northern Ireland of the 1920s out of guilt at what they had done during the Troubles: had done or perhaps had failed to do. (I don't know what the Brethren take is on 'omission' and 'commission', or any of the other divisions and gradations, although I have a vision of a single room with 'Sin' above the entrance in deepest red, and no back door.)* I thought, finally, about the man who sat in the armchair in my parents' living room on Sunday afternoons, after his wife died, drumming his fingers, saying little.

What if there was something more than a liking for a drink and a trip to the races locked away inside; more than just a child born out of wedlock to grapple with?

'The best man that ever lived,' Kate called him.

I did not doubt that he had become a better man in his later life. I just did not know how far short of good he had fallen in his earlier one.

---

* Actually I have just read the entry for sin in the 1917 *Catholic Encyclopaedia*. Call me a latecomer, but I don't know that I am any the wiser about their divisions and gradations either.

  That Brethren 'Sin' room, by the way . . . I think what I might be seeing is a version of the shed where the shipyard workers left their stolen tools.

Reckoning

'The 22nd of August will never be forgotten here. It will be
remembered like the "big wind".'
'Or the big fire.'*

When the clearing up began in Lisburn in the middle of the
week following Oswald Swanzy's murder, police discovered a
man's charred body in the burned-out shell of Donaghy's boot
factory. The head was missing, as was the left leg, although it
was assumed that the intense heat had caused this dismember-
ment and that the victim had been looting when the flames
overtook him. Even now information about the man's identity
is hard to come by. Of all the sources I consulted, the least
official, my Uncle David, again seemed the most reliable: a
down-and-out, was his memory, with no one to post him
missing, place a death notice, keep his name, at least, alive.

Despite the viciousness of the violence, the unpredictable
nature of fires once started, this is the only confirmed fatality in

* Exchange between solicitor and chairman of claims court, Lisburn court-
house, November 1920.

the fifty-odd hours of rioting in the town. The unrest meanwhile had spread to Belfast where at eight thirty-nine on the
morning of Friday 27th McNally's Spirit Grocer, otherwise 12
Templemore Street, was attacked and gutted. The fervency of
Eleanor's Unionism counted for nothing with the rioters set
against the fact that she had leased the bar to a Catholic.

   In all, twenty-two people were to lose their lives in the city
before the end of the month with a further five thousand
(mainly, but by no means exclusively, Catholic) forced to leave
their homes. The government imposed a ten-thirty curfew,
which remained in place until 1924. Lisburn's riots, that
'delirious nightmare' as the *Irish News* termed them, began
to seem less horrific in comparison, and as the years passed
merited less and less attention. They are not much more than a
footnote now.* Look in the index of books on that period of
Irish history and the chances are that the town's name will not
even appear. In fairness there is a lot of competition for space,
and not just from Belfast. The autumn of 1920 alone witnessed
the hanging in Dublin of Kevin Barry, the lad of eighteen
summers in the famous old ballad, and the murders, six
weeks before, of Privates Washington, Humphries and
Whitehead of the Duke of Wellington's West Riding
Regiment by Barry's ambush party;† witnessed too the first
Bloody Sunday, on which at least twenty-nine people died in

* Not that I have anything against footnotes.
† I once wrote an article comparing the stupid things I have done while
drunk with those I have done while stoned. The latter consisted mainly of
inappropriate laughter and repeat listenings to the piano line in Bob Dylan's
'I Want You'. The former included (would have included: I must have been
drunk when I started, for I never finished) the night I extemporised, to the
'Kevin Barry' air, the 'Ballad of One of the Shot Privates' on a minibus
carrying Irish writers from the Frankfurt Book Fair to   *cont'd over/*

the capital, a dozen of them shot by police in the middle of a Gaelic-football match between Dublin and Tipperary at Croke Park stadium; and the death on hunger strike of Terence MacSwiney, who had succeeded Tomás MacCurtain as both Lord Mayor of Cork and commander of the IRA in the city, and who at the time of his death was being held in Brixton Prison on charges of sedition.

A fortnight before Christmas Cork city itself was the headline-maker. Following an IRA ambush on a patrol of Auxiliary police at Dillon's Cross a night of reprisals began in the course of which Auxiliaries, Black and Tans, RIC men and regular troops (as drunk as the rest; like their being drunk matters in the scale of things) rampaged through the town, setting fire to the City Hall and a substantial part of Patrick Street, the main commercial district, where they also indulged in some serious looting. Once again the Great War was the touchstone for eyewitnesses. 'It was worse than if a fellow was out in France,' said one fireman, quoted by Gerry White and Brendan O'Shea in their book *The Burning of Cork*. The fireman had no way of knowing it, but the scenes actually anticipated the next war. You look at the photos, and there is no other word: this was *Blitzkrieg*.

All unnoticed, Lisburn recovered. Already the week after the riots its newspapers were carrying notices of fire-damage sales, of business as usual at temporary addresses. The tone is one of fortitude in the face of an unhappy accident. By the

† *cont'd*   their hotel. Before the end of the first verse a small, elderly and very irate, playwright had hurtled the length of the bus to confront me, tie wound tight around his fist. 'Apologise! Apologise!' (Even when they are losing the rag Irish writers of a certain vintage sound like they are quoting Joyce.)

middle of the next month the notices are of grand re-openings – the silver lining expanded almost to the size of the original cloud – although motorists are still being advised to drive slowly through the town at night lest they attract suspicion (or something infinitely worse) from the police.

At the end of September there was a renewed outbreak of violence arising from an incident at the Tuesday market in Market Square. Two townswomen got into an argument with a Catholic stallholder during which they claimed she called them 'Carson's pigs'. (I try, I really try, to imagine the sentence in which those words were uttered.) As in August, loyal citizens of Lisburn demonstrated their indignation by forcing entry into bars and attempting to make off with the contents. That night gangs smashed their way into three Catholic-owned houses on the County Down side of town, turfed the furniture out on to the street and burned it. The *Standard*, lamenting the cause of the trouble, said it came just as Catholics were moving back to the town and 'settling down quietly', never mind that the hardest thing any Catholic was alleged to have hurled that day was an insult ('Yous are a pair of Carson's pigs'? 'Away back to your Proddy sty with the rest of Carson's pigs'?), or for that matter that the *Standard*'s rival the *Herald* was adamant that Catholics had not left in any significant numbers to begin with.

The Tuesday after Swanzy's murder a reporter from the *Irish News* had called on the Roman Catholic Bishop of Down and Connor, the Most Reverend Dr MacRory, to ask him for a comment. His Lordship 'deeply deplored and most strongly condemned' the shooting. He stopped short, however, of saying he would write a letter to the press as he had done following the expulsion of Catholic workers from the shipyards and factories in July. A letter, he said, could be interpreted as an acknowledgment that some of his flock had been involved in the murder, something that he himself did not for a minute believe. Indeed, 'For all that he or the public knew the authors of the Lisburn tragedy might be Atheists or Nihilists and not Catholics at all; and he had no obligation – and certainly no desire – to assume at present that they were Catholics.'*

No one, it is true, had yet been charged, much less convicted, although arrests had already been made. Dr George St George, who had tended to Swanzy outside the Northern Bank, had somehow also had the presence of mind to make a note of the number plate of the taxi – OI 7345 – in which the District Inspector's killers made their getaway. It had been driven back into its Upper Library Street depot at four o'clock on the day of the murder, apparently none the worse for its 'jaunt along the coast'. (Clearly no one had thought to inspect the floor beneath the back seats.) That same evening Sean Leonard, the taxi driver, was taken into custody along with two north-Belfast brothers, John Vincent and James Joseph Montgomery. All three protested their innocence, Leonard now saying that he had been forced to drive up through Finaghy to a field in the townland of Poleglass (a large housing estate these days) and there to hand over his keys, his driving permit and his chauffeur's cap. For the next hour he was held at gunpoint by a hooded man who

* These Atheists and Nihilists were perhaps in league with the 'foreign agents' who, according to a spokesman for the United Kingdom Operative Plumbers' Society (Queen's Island branch) had been the real instigators of the expulsions the Bishop had previously condemned, going among 'their boys and girls' and inciting them to 'acts of rowdyism' that they would otherwise never have countenanced (*Irish News*, 28th August 1920).

instructed him, when the car had returned, to drive around for a while before going back to Belfast.

The Montgomery brothers were conditionally discharged in December, but Leonard was returned for trial and in February appeared before a special military court at Victoria Barracks, barely a click on the meter from Upper Library Street, and like Poleglass now a housing estate. Several eyewitnesses called before the tribunal identified him as a member of the murder gang, one of the gunmen, even, although whatever else he did that day Sean Leonard did not fire a gun. In her evidence one young girl, who had been leaving the cathedral with her mother just as the shooting started, said rather beautifully, although not altogether reliably, 'If I could not exactly swear to him I never saw a man more like him.' The owner of the Belfast Motor Cab and Engineering Company, on the other hand, said he had three drivers in the depot when the call came from 'Mr Brady' on the morning of 22nd August. It was quite by chance that Sean Leonard should have been in line to take the fare. As the defendant's lawyer said, he could as easily have ended up taking Edward Carson as an IRA gang, although it also emerged that Leonard had spent the hours before the call was received mending a puncture and so had not responded to earlier requests for bookings. Robert Lynch, who has written about the IRA in the North at that time, makes it quite clear that Joe McKelvey had 'arranged' it so that Leonard would be the driver.

The military court sentenced him to fifteen years for his part in the murder, the only person ever to be convicted.

*   *   *

Oswald Swanzy's mother and sister put in a claim for £15,000 damages, based on his annual earnings of £615 at the time of his death, his prospects for promotion (Chief Constable, predicted one colleague), and the fact that since his father and brother had died some years before Oswald had been the family's sole support. Local press condemned as 'a miserable pittance' the eventual award of £4,500. Two months later the court of appeal raised it to £6,000.

Peter McKeever, shot in the chest as he struggled to defend his Bridge Street bar, remained in hospital until the middle of December. He received an initial payment of fifty pounds although at a second hearing in July 1921 he was awarded a further thousand after evidence was given of the continued effects on his health and employment prospects. His left lung was 'entirely destroyed' and he would never again be able to do manual work. Already he had had to sell the bar that he had come back from Canada to run.

Mrs Gilmore, whose shop had been the first to be looted on 22nd August, had a rougher ride at her compensation claim for £2,377 stock-in-trade and furnishings: an over-inflated figure, the King's Counsel representing Lisburn Urban Council contested, and put it to the claimant that her losses in any case had been brought about by the 'performance of her son'. (There are bad reviews and then there are bad reviews.) Mrs Gilmore told the court how she had had to jump from a rear window into the graveyard when the mob broke in at the front and how even then she had been pursued and threatened with being shot. When asked why she had not yet returned to the town she broke down in tears. She would not go back now, she said bitterly, for all the money she ever handled.

William Shaw the Sinn Fein councillor smuggled out of the County Infirmary under a waterproof sheet was awarded twenty-five pounds for injuries sustained in the beating that landed him in there in the first place. Argument in court centred on the movement in one of his little fingers: how much he had had before 22nd August, how much he had had since, how much, come to that, a person really needed.

So numerous were the claims that proceedings had to be transferred to the County Court in Belfast, starting at the end of November. Early in the New Year the Recorder, Judge Matheson, announced that he would not hear any more cases after 13th February. At the beginning of that week, however, almost eighty of the three hundred and twenty cases had still not been dealt with. (The definitive figure, quoted in court, for properties wrecked or burned was 287, but there was often more than one claim per property.) For some the court ordeal cannot have been much less traumatic or invasive than the destruction of their homes and businesses.

James Douglas, a father of twelve from Bridge Street, was claiming five hundred pounds in lost furniture. The King's Counsel quizzed him on the size of his house.

'Is the front of your house nine feet six inches broad?'

'Yes.'

'It was a kitchen house?'

'Yes.'

'How many bedrooms?'

'Two with five beds in them.'

'And with five hundred pounds of furniture in a kitchen house where did you put the children?'

'In the beds.'

Cue gales of laughter in the court.

He walked away with four hundred pounds less than he had been hoping for.

Harriet Convery, a widow of Longstone Street, claiming for, among other effects, thirty pounds in damaged books, including an Irish history, was told by Judge Matheson that books were sold by the yard in Dublin . . . 'By the ton,' King's Counsel added helpfully.

The judge returned to his theme when a valuation of £150 was put on the books lost in the burning of St Patrick's parochial house. The housekeeper testified that she had seen several *Lives of the Saints* in the house: 'big heavy books with gold lines on them', although she could not say who had written them. Judge Matheson informed the woman that his own library was estimated to be worth £1,500, but that he would be happy if he got £200 for it.

'There is nothing,' he concluded, 'which depreciates so much in value as clerical books, Irish histories, and law books.'

On another occasion he interrupted proceedings to ask whether *all* the coal scuttles in Lisburn were made of mahogany.

No matter what the figure first mentioned an expert could always be produced to drive it down. (OK, it was a court; it's what they do.) Countering the claim that the parochial house itself would cost two shillings and sixpence per square foot to rebuild, Mr H. Martin, of H & J Martin, builders, wagered that he could 'rebuild Lisburn, or any part of it' for one-and-eight a square foot. Which, coming from the man whose company had in the recent past built Belfast's City Hall, to budget and on time, was always going to carry a bit of weight with Judge Matheson.*

In general awards came out at about a quarter of the amount claimed. Daniel Mooney, owner of the Empire Hotel on Chapel Hill, fared better than most. He had taken in Belgian refugees during the war, for which service he had received letters of thanks from the Belgian and British governments. These letters were destroyed in the arson attack on his business, along with his son's stamp collection: three thousand stamps valued at £150. (Not a peep of protest from Judge Matheson, the old philatelist.) He was awarded £5,250 of £11,186 claimed.

Some of the claims were, for their time, enormous – eighty thousand pounds in the case of Donaghy's boot factory – and some of the settlements heartbreakingly modest: thirteen pounds to Emily Toole of 42 Chapel Hill, ten pounds to John Hegarty of number 58, who had hidden with his neighbour in a cellar during the attack. Patrick Gallagher, hairdresser, was awarded six pounds for damage to his business, Katie Bullick of Longstone Street received just two pounds to cover the cost of replacing her broken windows.

Emily Toole never moved back into 42 Chapel Hill, but settled much more modestly in Stewart's Court, through a

---

* Work on the City Hall started in 1898 and was completed eight years later at a cost of £360,000, of which nearly £40,000 was spent on sculpture and ornamentation. Brett and Patton are, as ever, your best guides, right down to the 'brisk moustache' on the statue to the Marquis of Dufferin and Ava (Patton) and the 'frolicsome little temple . . . in which he is enshrined' (Brett). H & J Martin is still going strong. The City Hall, though, is taking a breather. At time of writing it is closed for a two-year refurbishment. Subsidence. Well, there has been a lot of stomping around in there down the decades.

low archway between her old house and number 44. Her neighbour in the court (number one to Emily's three), as on Chapel Hill, was Mary Jane Logue. She could hardly have 'settled down' any more quietly than in that little out-of-the-way place.*

Mary Jane's name does not appear anywhere in the long list of compensation claimants, perhaps because (and you could probably have made as long a list again of such cases) she had not filed for damages within the three-day period required by law.

Again I found myself asking where she was during those three days, where Kate and Eileen were.

Again I wanted to ask Jack, 'What were you doing, Granddad?'

Even *thinking* rhetorically it was hard sometimes to keep the edge out of my voice.

Eileen never spoke to her brothers, or her children, about that time: it belonged 'behind the curtain' with the circumstances of her conception and birth. Nor did the curtain lift – twitch even – in the long years of her dementia, when a loosening of the grip on the distinction between then and now might be expected, all involuntarily, to occur. However she held on to them, at whatever the cost, she took her memories to the grave. Eventually.

* Fred Kee, the sanitary inspector turned local historian, writes of the total lack of privacy in an entry like Stewart's Court. Whenever he visited one of the houses all the other occupants would come out to see what was going on.

Couples

Eleanor Patterson, née Spence, erst(a little)while Davis, had been suffering from chronic gastritis for a year before she succumbed to a heart attack in the third week of January 1925. Jack was with her at the end and was on hand a few days later to amend her death certificate and reconcile her finally to her age. Her estate, much of it in furniture, quite a bit of it in the chiffonier, came to forty-three pounds and three shillings, or something under a tenth of what had been left to her by Phares thirty years before. Jack, her sole beneficiary, also inherited the houses in Templemore Street, a part of his father's legacy that Eleanor had for some reason never touched: some very good reason, you might say, given her track record. Much had changed in Belfast since the houses were built, and little of it for the better. The houses were actually worth less in 1925 than they were back in the early 1890s and never again recovered their value.

Jack nonetheless spent thirteen pounds and eight shillings on his mother's funeral, specifying best cloth coffin, superior upholstery, best nightdress, ribbon and hose. He spent a further seventy pounds the following year on a granite enclosure for the grave in which she was buried next to her first, and, so far as the family history was concerned, her only, husband. Jack was married himself by then, of course. In fact the wedding had followed so hard on the heels of the funeral that I seriously wondered whether it was the announcement of the former, and not chronic gastritis, which brought on the heart attack that led to the latter.

After a decade of living apart Jack and Kate now settled down to have the family that Eleanor had denied them. With four boys born in the next eleven years, and two miscarriages besides, Kate did not return to the mill, but took part-time work when the boys were up a bit, cleaning for the 'big people' off the Antrim Road. Never anything less than cheerful, she was, to use one of Northern Ireland's greatest compliments 'very well thought of' by her various employers. Many of the clothes she dressed her sons in were hand-me-downs from these big people's own no-longer-quite-so-small ones. My father mentions in particular a pair of sailor suits that saw service on David and Jackie's backs before they were handed down again to him and Edmund. David would not have been long out of his sailor suit when, at the height of the Great Depression, Kate sent him down the street with a basket of food for a widowed neighbour with a family to feed. You accepted what you were given without shame and gave what you could without stint.

By the time Edmund was born in March 1936 Eileen was approaching twenty-one. On 2nd October 1937 she married Jamesie Smylie, who was ten years older again.

Jamesie had grown up on McKeown Street, which opened off Antrim Street, just before its junction with Bachelors Walk. His father was a cobbler whose first wife, Jamesie's mother, died while Jamesie was still an infant. Her sister Lizzie was married to John Wylie. It was that size of a town.

Right from the start there were problems with Eileen and Jamesie's marriage. Jamesie was a street fighter and a drinker, a lethal combination, even if fights outside bars on a Friday night back then were practically a spectator sport. (The court reporters would suspend their censoriousness, coming over all Damon Runyon.) He boxed more formally – became in fact a featherweight champion – in the army, which he joined at the outbreak of the Second World War.* He served in the South-East Asian Theatre and signed up again on demobilisation, after which he was stationed, less exotically, in the north-west of Ulster. Ella, his first child, born in 1941, spent so much of her early life with Jack and Kate that she would tell people she had two daddies, her Real Daddy and her Soldier Daddy. (By the same token Edmund always looked on her as more of a little sister than a niece.) When Jamesie came home for one spell of leave Ella accidentally burned her hand in the fire in her upset at seeing him and her Real Daddy in the same room.

Eileen had wanted to call her daughter Catherine (the name Kathleen was strictly for the wedding day and after February

* Northern Ireland's pre-eminent boxers have all tended to be 'wee men': Rinty Monaghan, Wayne McCullough, Barry McGuigan; flyweight, bantamweight, featherweight. It is OK to call a wee man 'Wee Man', by the way, although given their pedigree you would maybe want to make sure you did it politely. I am six foot, dead. I get 'Big Man' at least once a day. See footnote to p. 60.

1925 was never heard again).* Kate would have none of
it.

'I know what will happen,' she said. 'You'll get in a fuss
one day and cast it back at me: "I'm sorry I ever named that
child after you." '

The family colouring, the fiery temper.

It was Kate who suggested Eleanor as an alternative, a
double-edged compliment if ever there was one, as much as
to say if you are going to cast anything back you can cast it
back at her.

Everyone I talked to told me the same thing: Eileen had a
'hard time'. Jamesie did not always unclench his fists when he
got out of the ring, or when he rolled in off the street,
victorious but still the worse for wear. There were many times
when his drinking left the family virtually penniless. Edmund in particular bailed his sister out on more than one
occasion. And then her second child, Jim, needed extra care
as a baby. It was not just Ella's own preference that saw her so
often over the road in number 9. Even now when she uses the
first-person plural in relation to those years she is more often
than not referring to her and Jack and Kate.

'We lived very frugally,' she says, but Jack, who chewed
every mouthful twenty times, 'made a feast out of nothing'.

It is not an empty phrase. Meat was bought in small

---

* Or so I thought until I went to Edmund and Isobel's golden anniversary
dinner, and there was a photograph of her, arriving at the church, spring
1958 – hat, no Jack – and there was her name in the church registry:
Kathleen. Maybe she just kept it for best. (The church, incidentally,
Magheradrool, is the one mentioned on p. 24, that hangout for 'disorderly
persons', that 'very aceldama' of an excitable Victorian press. You would
never guess it looking at the photos: the very acme of orderliness and
wedding-day joy.)

quantities as it was needed or could be afforded, with Kate off across to the butcher at the top of Antrim Street at eight in the morning. Chances are she tried to get him to knock a bit of money off. She was another haggler – if anything a more determined one than Jack. So well known for it was she, my father swears, that the greengrocer, seeing her coming, would put a penny on his oranges knowing he would end up having to take it off again.

(Her distrust of recommended prices and her need to be careful with money could be taken to even more comic extremes. She was once asked to price the goods on the cake stall at my father's Church Lads' Brigade fête. She did it gladly, but when the fête opened walked past the stall without buying anything. 'I wouldn't pay the like of that,' she said.)

Stew, with mutton, and soup were staples. Ella would be sent every Sunday with bowls of one or the other to 'Wee Billy' and 'Wee Maggie', Kate's brother and widowed sister, who lived three doors apart in Stewart's Court. Billy had lived in number 1 with his mother until her death in 1935 then with his brother Tommy until the latter's marriage. They were tiny, the Stewart's Court houses, closer to cottages. Maggie's in particular, at the very bottom of the court, was to Ella's eyes little better than a hovel. Ella would find her sitting just inside the door with a black shawl over her head and a fire burning summer and winter, her thoughts who knows where between there and the cemetery in France where her husband's body lay. Maggie was less literate even than Kate. Her war widow's pension book lived behind one of the china dogs on the mantelpiece in Antrim Street. She would pick it up each Monday morning on her way to the

post office, still in her shawl, and Jack would sign his name
beside her mark. Despite her surname, O'Neill, being clearly
printed on the pension book's cover, Jack never referred to
her as anything other than the 'Wee Woman Neill'.

Young as she was, Ella knew that Billy and Maggie were
both Catholic, from which it followed that Kate must be, or
at least must have been, Catholic too. And yet she remembers
being brought up – being brought up to all intents and
purposes in 9 Antrim Street – with the understanding that it
did not do to get too involved with Catholics. It is, she
recognises, a conundrum and one that fifty years later she is
no nearer to solving.

There was, of course, colouring everything, Jack's new-
born faith. All past thoughts and actions were now subject
to reflection and repentance. Ella's memory like mine is of
a man who said little. (My memory of her Soldier Daddy
is of a man who, if anything, said even less. Jamesie
smiled more, though, perhaps because it didn't take as
much effort as speaking.) Quiet rather than stern, is her
verdict, and for all his willing observance capable of small
acts of defiance. After one particularly bitter schism, in
1959, the Exclusive Brethren came under the control of
'Big Jim' Taylor Jr. who instructed members not to take
their meals with non-believers, as though being in the
presence of those not 'washed in the blood' would somehow contaminate their food. In the case of one family in
the Antrim Street fellowship this meant an un-saved
brother being sent out to a shed to eat. Jack, however,
carried on as before, sitting down at the table with Kate
and Ella, and whoever else Kate had invited in off the
street, chewing every mouthful twenty times. Soon after-

wards he cut his ties with the meeting hall across the road – making a leper of himself rather than make lepers of his family – and joined a less paranoid assembly in the gloomy building I remember in Belfast's bedsit land.* Likewise, although he had long since resigned from Lisburn Conservative, he still wrote out scores for the Hillhall Flute Band, in which Jackie, Edmund and my father all played. (The connection to Hillhall was presumably through the McKeavenys, Mary Jane's Protestant siblings and their families.) He also kept a miniature keyboard on which he composed hymn tunes. And he would still play the flute himself when called on, and of course sing 'If Those Lips Could Only Speak' to send Wee Billy Bingham home with a tear in his eye.

He had few material ambitions. Again Ella could not help but notice the disparity between his standard of living and his brothers'. Going to see William, who had moved the short distance from Derry up the coast to Whiterocks, near Portrush, on his retirement, was 'like visiting royalty'. David too had prospered. His Lisburn Road shop had proved to be a 'little goldmine', which was still minting money in the 1970s when I was at grammar school down the road, although David was dead by then and his son-in-law managing the shop. It had bought David a very nice house in

---

* As you can tell from the words 'control' and 'instructed' there had been a shift away from the notion of 'all saints alike': Big Jim was variously 'Angel' and the 'Elect Vessel'. He was discovered in bed with a woman church member – a mother of four – in Aberdeen in 1970, occasioning yet another split, despite his claims that they had retreated there to have a sandwich in safety. (Well, I would have tried it.) He died the following year, somewhat predictably an alcoholic.

which to see out his days, on Adelaide Park off the famously well-heeled Malone Road.*

Fred had become a master bleacher, working in mills and research institutes the length and breadth of Northern Ireland. His notes on innovations in the bleaching process you will find – if you look under P. Patterson, not F. – in the Public Records Office in Belfast. You will find there too a photo of him in cricket whites, his army-reserve discharge papers, a diary presented to him by his sister Aggie in 1908 and completed in code (although the words 'Maze races' jump out at you in plain English) and a piece of self-regarding doggerel entitled 'There's Patterson (Hurrah, Hurroo)':

> Some people thought it was his Ar__
> That they were pointing at
> But that's because they had none themselves
> And they wore it under their hats.

There is a second diary, from 1917, containing little more than football scores and team sheets, in many of which Fred's name appears (the year after the discharge on medical grounds). The diary has been doodled on by Fred's daughter, also Ella, probably around 1930, certainly before she started

* Many of these houses too were in time divided into flats. I lived in one of them in the first part of 1989 before moving to Lisburn. At the top end of the street was the derelict Aquinas Hall, formerly the residence of the Church of Ireland Bishop of Down, Connor and Dromore, previously mentioned, where Louis MacNeice is supposed to have written 'Snow'. At the bottom end was the first-floor flat where Robert McLiam Wilson definitely did write *Eureka Street*. I watched him do it. We all did. It was the way he liked to work. Some days there was a queue down the stairs and out into the garden. No cable then, of course. No online shopping.

ALL GOODS RECEIVED ARE SUBJECT TO TERMS & CONDITIONS
IN BLEACHERS' AND FINISHERS' ASSOCIATION PRICE LIST.

· ESTABLISHED 1626 ·

LAMBEG BLEACHING, DYEING & FINISHING CO. LTD.

BLEACHERS · DYERS · FINISHERS

TELEGRAMS-FINISH, LISBURN.
TELEPHONES-LISBURN 2617(2 LINES)

LAMBEG,
LISBURN.
NORTHERN IRELAND.

26th March, 1964.

Dear Jack,

Due to the closure of the Works you are leaving the Company
to-day after almost 50 years of service. During this long period
of time you have carried out your duties with the greatest degree
of faithfulness and integrity and have earned the highest esteem
of your fellow employees and of management. On behalf of the
Directors I would therefore like you to accept the very best thanks
of all, together with the enclosed cheque, and I sincerely hope
that you will have a long and happy retirement.

Yours very sincerely,

Director.

Jack Patterson, Esq.,

school, to judge by the arms growing out of the heads of the
people she drew. Ella died in 1941, aged fourteen, and was
buried in the family plot on Merchants' Row. My father
vividly recalls walking with Jack to Moore's Bridge to meet
the cortège coming in from Bellievy, near Banbridge, where
Fred was then in charge of the bleaching department.

It would break your heart, that diary.

Jack, a scholar still at eighteen, remained at the lower end of the skills and wages scale all his working life. From Glenmore Bleach Works he moved to the Lambeg Bleaching, Dyeing and Finishing Company — Bleach Green for short — where he put in fifty years as a cloth passer, leaving only when the Bleach Green closed down in 1963. He was lucky to make it that far. A couple of years after the end of the war a blood vessel burst in his brain while he was lifting a bale of cloth. The works doctor who first examined him gave him next to no chance of survival. It was his own son David who pressed for him to be placed in a head brace packed around with ice (David had clearly picked up a lot more than tittle-tattle about his grandmother in his rounds of the town). Thus was Jack saved a second time.

Unable to move at all to begin with, he was off work in the end for six weeks, the longest period of ill health he ever experienced. The Brethren supplemented his sick pay. 'A fiver a week,' my father hazards from memory. If it was anything close to that then it was extremely generous and makes up a little for the lunacy of banishing non-believers from the dinner table: Jack's settlement on the closure of the Bleach Green was two hundred and fifty pounds, or a fiver a year.

His final job, which he kept until he was well into his seventies, was one David had created for him at his wholesale firm in Belfast. I have a dim recollection of seeing him, in his waistcoat and collarless shirt, waiting to catch my brothers and me as we slid down the chute from the first-floor stores. Warehouse helper was the official job description. It was something for him to do, but it was also a way for David to help his parents out financially without it looking like charity. (The settlement from the Bleach Green apart Jack had no works pension to speak of.) Besides, when you consider Kate's largesse with his gifts of groceries there is no saying that if he had simply given them money she would not have stood on the doorstep handing out shillings to passers-by.

'There you are, Man. There you are, Woman. Don't spend it all in the one shop.'

She had once told my mother she wished she had her brother-in-law William's money 'to give to all of you', and could not fathom why the attic at Clarendon Street, and later Whiterocks, was stuffed full of perfectly good furniture. What was the point of having it if no one ever got see it, much less use it?

There may, though, have been something more than just an earth mother's bountiful instincts behind these sentiments. Despite the appearance of her will, Eleanor had until relatively late in her life control of, or an interest in, a substantial amount of property, some of which might well have accrued to her from her second marriage, and all of which was divvied up, it seems, with the minimum of paperwork. William inherited a large house in the suburban Knock area of east Belfast. The bar on that side of town – the one that had survived the 1920 riots – went to Emma's widower, Jim Moneypenny, and so on.

'The rest of them got the plums,' Kate told her children. 'Your father got Templemore Street at five shillings a week.'

All the same, she was grateful for the quarterly rent cheque from the solicitor. She used it to wipe clean the slates she had run up with shopkeepers about the town in the previous three months. These shopkeepers did her a further good turn, providing work for each of her sons as soon as they hit their ninth birthday. (It wasn't pocket money they were working for.) My father was presented at Turner's fruit and vegetable shop on

Bow Street in April 1941, a matter of days after seven hundred people had perished in the first major German air raid on Belfast.*

'There's a new errand boy for you,' Kate said, and when the shopkeeper thanked her – because how else was he supposed to respond? – told him not to mention it: 'I'll have another one for you in a few years' time.'

A few years after that again my father walked out the gates of his school, Lisburn Central, for the last time.† The following Monday morning he walked in the gates of the Northern Ireland Road Transport Board directly opposite the school and began work as an apprentice sheet-metal worker.

So he was practically a veteran when, at the age of nineteen, he went out on the town in Belfast with his friend Bertie Neill, Old Year's Night 1951, and, after trying one ballroom without success (oh, come on, what other kind of success could I possibly mean?), and getting a pass out for a drink, found his way up the stairs to Sammy Leckey's Dance Studio on Royal Avenue.

A whole new round of begetting was about to begin.

---

* There was an air-raid shelter, with seating for forty, right outside the door of 9 Antrim Street. Jack was entrusted with the key. It was a surprise to me that shelters had keys. It would be no surprise to me if he and Kate had gone into their particular shelter every so often and given it a dust and a clean.
† Lisburn Central had replaced the town's plethora of church schools in the early thirties, a time of great expansion in the primary school sector in Northern Ireland. My own Finaghy Primary dates from this time, as does Strandtown Primary in east Belfast whose football pitches my study overlooks. My father never takes in the view without remembering the time he came up here with his church-schools-united team to play against a team containing Jackie Blanch-flower, soon to be one of Manchester United's Busby Babes, but looking to my father then like a full-grown man in a team of full-grown men. 'Six–nil down at half time,' my father says, as though he still can't quite believe it.

A Long Chapter, Happy then Sad

'He went out to get a Babycham,' is how my mother's version of meeting my father runs, 'and he found me.'

Even if you do not know Babycham, or my mother, you have to say that is a pretty good deal. If you do know Babycham, you will know that it wasn't launched nationally until 1953, although it had been bottled since 1950, when it was product-tested in the Bristol area. For once it looks as though Belfast was way ahead of the rest of the country.*

Well, the Elephant Bar was.

That is where my father and Bertie Neill had stopped between ballrooms, a house known for its Guinness-and-Babycham. My father's version is heavier on the Guinness.

* If I tell you this is from the Babycham website it is not to pretend to no knowledge of my own. I once drank four bottles of the stuff before school after the girl I was going out with dumped me, or at least dangled me for the umpteenth time (see p. 5 and for that matter p. 180). I was in the upper sixth, in the process of failing my Oxbridge entrance exam, and only semi-attached to the school. A very understanding English teacher stopped me in the corridor that morning and told me to wise up and go home. As tales of excess go, I realise, it falls a little short of shooting up in the toilets of the Prime Minister's private jet.

My mother had not long arrived at Sammy Leckey's with her friend Meta (her brother's former fiancée, in fact) when my father came in and asked could he and Bertie have the next dance.

'Sure you can,' said Meta who sounds from the sarky tone my mother gives her as though she may have been linking my mother's arm at the time. But they danced the dance anyway, Meta with my father, Bertie with my mother, then they swapped over for the dance after that and didn't swap back. They were still dancing together when it came time for my mother and Meta to go for their buses.

(This was Old Year's Night, a different animal altogether from New Year's Eve.)

They arranged, all four, to go to the pictures that Wednesday: *City Lights*, at the Classic. My mother laughed so much she thought, there is no way this fella is ever going to ask me out again. But that was just what he did as they walked to the bus: 'What about Saturday night?' It was not until the next day that she realised, talking to Meta, that he had not been asking her on a double date. By the time Saturday night came, Bertie Neill would already be back in London, where he had just signed professional forms with Tottenham Hotspur. (He had been wearing his Spurs blazer on Old Year's Night. He told Meta it was from his old public school. She fell for it, as my mother fell for his reference to my father as a Big Wheel. Fell or let herself fall.) My mother was thrown into a panic. She was only two months past her seventeenth birthday: she had never done the like of this in her life before. Still, the arrangement had been made and – he lived in Lisburn, he had no telephone (so much for the Big Wheel) – there was no way to unmake it. And she could hardly leave the fella standing, could she?

She went.

The Imperial this time, but Chaplin again, in *Limelight*, 'I'll be loving you eternally' and all that impossible-to-resist jazz.

They were in their second year of courtship when Annie and Billy, my mother's parents, decided to go out to Canada to live. Annie had been once before, in the 1920s.* Billy had, almost literally, washed up there for a few weeks in the Second World War after his merchant-navy vessel was torpedoed in the North Atlantic. He went out again in April 1953 and Annie followed in October with their six-year-old son Gordon.

My mother and father travelled with them as far as Dublin, where Annie and Gordon caught the train to Cobh and the ship to take them to Montreal. The plan was that my mother would stay on in Belfast, going to live with her grandmother, my Great-granny Coates, who was minding the house, off the Woodvale Road, in which I would one day lodge the grandmother of Drew Linden, doppelganger of my ex-girlfriend's crush and central character of *Fat Lad*. Within a

---

* She was seventeen. When her mother refused to help her with her passage she went round to the British Legion and showed them the dog tags she had smuggled out of the house. Her father, George Corr, was another of the First World War fallen: day one, the Somme. The Legion gave her the fare and ten pounds to tide her over till she found a job. She wound up in Saskatoon with a Scots Catholic girl, May McKay, she befriended on the boat. They stuck together for two years (almost literally: Saskatoon felt like the coldest place on earth) before a letter arrived from Belfast. It contained Annie's ticket home. 'If it had been money,' she says, 'I'd have sent it back, but my mother had gone to all that trouble.' May took over her old job in a doctor's surgery and a short time later married the doctor's son.

matter of days, however, a letter arrived with the news that Gordon had been taken seriously ill with acidosis halfway across the Atlantic. The ship had had to put in at Halifax, Nova Scotia, for him to get proper medical treatment. My mother didn't think twice: she had to go out and help take care of him. My father didn't even think: he was going with her.

There was great consternation in Antrim Street when he made the announcement, and it wasn't lessened any when my father arranged to lodge, for a time, with Kate's brother Dan and his wife Margaret, who had emigrated some years before and were living in Toronto fifty miles from the town of Galt where Annie and Billy had settled. Then again, you can see Jack and Kate thinking, what is fifty miles when you have already travelled three thousand?

They had a point. Just a few months after he and my mother sailed, on the *Queen Mary*, in the spring of 1954, my father was writing home to say that they were to be married that coming July. A letter arrived by return, from Jack (naturally), offering not congratulations but advice: 'Make sure you know what you are doing.' Angry and hurt, my father sat down at once to pen his reply. My mother, looking on, puzzled over one particular line:

'I'm surprised at you especially,' it said.

More than two decades later, reflecting on her heart-to-heart with Kate in 9 Antrim Street, she wondered whether my father might not after all have had some suspicion of the truth of his own parents' marriage, although my father maintains he had none at all and was simply upbraiding Jack on what he considered an un-Christian response.

The letter in any case was never sent. The wedding went ahead, in Galt. It goes without saying that Jack and Kate were not there, but then the wedding could have taken place in any church in Lisburn and it would go without saying that at least one of them would not have been there.

My brothers, Brian, Paul and Kevin, were born in little more than three and a half years, beginning February 1955, and looked set fair to grow up as all-Canadian boys. There was any amount of work for my father, an expanding circle of friends for him and my mother, including one friend, Reggie Teeny, who had lived a couple of doors along from Eileen on Antrim Street; and then there was just *Canada*, the ease of it all after post-war Northern Ireland. My father, though, never entirely got over the homesickness that had struck him – rendered him almost inconsolable – on the voyage west.*

The tipping point, my mother is in no doubt, was the arrival of a tape from Lisburn – it seems to have been Edmund's idea – with relatives and members of the repertory company shouting their hellos into the microphone and swelling the choruses of sentimental Irish ballads:

> Oh the roof was thatched with yellow straw
> And the walls were white as snow
> And the turf fire boiled the pot, I see it still.
> [Rep. company echo: *I see it still . . .*]

---

* It couldn't have helped much that there was a storm the second night out and that the liner had to weigh anchor until it had passed. There was a tugboat strike as well, so instead of arriving in New York the *Queen Mary* had diverted to Halifax, which was clearly to transatlantic liners what Lisburn was to Northern Irish trains.

What defence was it against such tugs on the heartstrings to point out that there was no Little Old Mud Cabin on this particular Hill, or that the backyard of the house where the tape was being made was filled with the coal that kept the Modern Mistress Range boiling the pots?

In fairness to my father, I suppose, this would have been the first time he had heard even his own parents' voices since leaving Lisburn four years before. He stuck it out in Galt for a year and a half more before prevailing on my mother to come back home and give Northern Ireland another go. It was the end of the 1950s, a new era. Things were starting to look up there too. What could go wrong?

Almost the first thing he had to do was go to a funeral. The day that the ship carrying the family of five docked in Belfast, Billy Logue, Kate's brother, died. God help you, Hughie McClinton, bereft for ever of a friend to lead off with.

I was born two years later. I would like to be able to sustain the new-era metaphor by telling you, as I was often told, that I was named for America's first astronaut Colonel John Glenn, but as he did not go into orbit until February 1962 I will concede that it is more likely, as I was just as often told, that my name came by way of Glenn Ford, who in 1961 was starring in *Cry for Happy* and *Pocketful of Miracles*.

Mind you, *Cry for Happy* . . . *Miracles* . . . they are not bad associations for a child to bring with him into the world. Better certainly than anything in Ford's 1962 output: *The Four Horsemen of the Apocalypse* and *Experiment in Terror*.

Billy Logue's brother Dan died in Toronto in the autumn of 1970. My parents took my brothers and me to Canada the following summer for their first trip back in twelve years. They had been saving up for it for at least a quarter of that time. Work might not have been a problem for a man with a trade here in the 1960s, but for a couple with four children money always was.

In the second week of the holiday my father drove us the fifty miles from Galt to see Dan's widow Margaret, who served us macaroni cheese, so alien and exotic that none of us four boys – so meat-and-two-veg Irish – could manage more than a mouthful.

We bought pastel-striped jeans, donned head-to-toe rubberised capes to walk behind Niagara Falls, and hung out with our bearded Uncle Gordon, who had had the brush with death on the boat from Cobh, and his pretty, long-haired wife Sue: as hippy-looking a couple as we had ever seen. (For Christmas 1971 they sent us The Mamas and the Papas' *Greatest Hits* and *The Best of the Guess Who*. Man, but I thought we were so *hip*.) The arrival home this time coincided with the introduction of internment in Northern Ireland: 342 arrests and fourteen deaths in twenty-four hours.* Just about anything that could have gone wrong here in the decade between Billy and Dan Logue dying had gone wrong.

In the days before her death from ovarian cancer in February 1972, Kate told visitors she had seen Dan looking through the window of her room in the Lagan Valley Hospital. A short time later she told my father that Jamesie Smylie had been in to see her. Jamesie had died three weeks earlier in another of the Lagan Valley's cancer wards (his lungs), but word of his death had been kept from Kate for fear of upsetting her more.

---

* Saturday 9th August 1971. It was my tenth birthday. I stood in my striped jeans at the back bedroom window of our house in Finaghy watching the smoke rising from identical housing estates a mile or so to the west. I had never felt so well travelled, so world-weary.

She was not a bit pleased to be in hospital – was proud of never having needed one in her life till then, or a dentist for that matter, always preferring to deal with troublesome teeth herself. The little woman lying in the Lagan Valley, waving to Dan, chatting to Jamesie, had barely a tooth left in her head. And she was still, to Jack, the greatest in Lisburn.

Closer to the end she saw an angel too, standing at the foot of the bed. No fairies, I am a little sorry to say.

Her coffin was lowered into the ground beside the coffins of Phares, Jack's father; Phares, Jack's nephew; Ella, Jack's niece; Agnes, Jack's 'Auntie McNeill'; and of course – nine parts funeral, one part parable – Jack's mother, Eleanor.

In September 1972 the widow and the widower, Eileen and Jack, moved with Eileen's son Jim into 4 Eagle Terrace, about half a mile from Lisburn town centre, just before the start of the Low Road. The Low Road was Jack's least favourite road in all of Lisburn, but Eagle Terrace was also the largest house he had lived in since Smithfield at the start of the Great War. The first he had owned too. He had been in Antrim Street for fifty-seven years, paying rent. It was fifty-three pence, or ten and a half shillings, a week when he left. In the early 1950s, when the rent was three shillings less, Edmund, a Northern Ireland Youth International, signed semi-professional forms with Portadown Football Club for a fee of four hundred pounds. The first thing he did was contact his parents' landlord who told him the house could be bought outright for two hundred pounds. Edmund took the train to Belfast with the money in his coat pocket only to find that the price had leaped while he travelled to eight hundred pounds. However all those seven-and-sixes stacked up, the landlord had clearly decided on reflection it was not in his interest to sell.

Not long afterwards Newcastle United, then at the height of their fame, made a move to bring Edmund across the water to St James's Park. It was big back-page news for a few days in the Northern Irish papers, but Newcastle's interest cooled when the club realised Edmund was already semi-pro, and would therefore command a cash transfer fee. (It wasn't unusual then for players to move for a new set of kits, a year's supply of match balls.) Eventually the deal fell through; which made two thwarted dreams involving the same sum of money.*

There had been car-bomb attacks in the centre of Lisburn in the months leading up to September 1972, with Bow Street in particular – only yards at its nearest point from 9 Antrim Street – badly knocked about. The *Ulster Star*, whose own office was on the street, dubbed it Bomb Alley. (No town in Northern Ireland then was complete without one.) Lisburn once more resembled the town that in August 1920 resembled war-torn France, but, although there were individual instances, there was no repeat of the wholesale sectarian violence that had erupted back then and that was again afflicting Belfast.†

* Edmund remained at Portadown for the rest of his career and later became chief scout under the management of Bertie Neill, who had returned to Northern Ireland after spells at Stoke and Oldham as assistant to Jimmy McIlroy. Bertie had married Jimmy's sister, Doreen: that old public-school-blazer charm.
† Neither was there in Lisburn anything like the same incidence of doorstep assassinations, which made those early-1970s nights in Belfast such nerve-shredding affairs. There were, however, numerous fatal beatings and stabbings down the years in and around the town centre. In the early hours of 18th March 1991, to take just one example, a month before the murder of Ernest McCrum, a gang of Protestant youths, linked to the UVF, stabbed seventeen-year-old Catholic Francis Taggart sixty-two times as he took a short cut home behind the leisure centre. And the 'combatants' wonder why so many people here do not share their view that this was a war.

Jack's second eldest son, my Uncle Jackie, was in the thick of the mayhem. He had trained as a butcher and worked for a time in the army stores at Sprucefield, on the southern outskirts of Lisburn. He had also, though, spent a period in the police (by now the RUC) at the end of the 1950s during the short-lived IRA 'border campaign'. (It had consisted in the main of gun attacks on rural police stations, most of them part-time and frequently, when attacked, empty.) When that fizzled out, Jackie joined the Ulster Special Constabulary, brought into being during the Troubles of 1920: brought into being in no small part in response to the violence in Lisburn, although perversely not so much to protect people from arson and looting, as to remove the need for loyal citizens to take the law into their own hands, as they were seen to have been forced to do then. Originally there had been three grades of special constable: A (full-time), B (part-time) and C (reserve); but A and C were phased out soon after the Second World War. The remaining B Specials – often just referred to as the Specials – were Protestant almost to a man. (Women? You're kidding, right?)

I have a memory of Jackie coming into the bedroom I shared with two of my brothers when I was a kid and showing us a newspaper – the *Orange Telegraph* or some such (they were as ephemeral as fanzines) – glorifying the attack, at the isolated Burntollet Bridge, on a civil rights march from Belfast to Derry in the opening days of January 1969. Off-duty members of the Specials had mingled with the attackers and even, all the history books agree, directed them, although it is debatable how much direction you would need to throw rocks at a bunch of unarmed marchers, or wade into them wielding clubs studded with nails.

If he was not there in body, and I did not get the impression that he was, Jackie was certainly there in spirit. That was the meaning of showing us the newspaper: this was the stuff to give those civil rights people!*

---

* Strictly speaking it was a People's Democracy (PD) march in support of civil rights, but without the backing of the Northern Ireland Civil Rights Association itself. A few dozen PD members – students for the most part – had set off from Belfast City Hall early on New Year's morning. I got talking one night at dinner a year or so ago to a woman who had been there and who put the numbers starting out as low as ten. She had met her husband-to-be on the march, although not on that first morning. He had been up till all hours the night before and travelled by bus to meet up with the marchers in Antrim. He was on hand, though, at Burntollet to help get her off the road, away from the rocks and flailing clubs. We clinked glasses, 'I think my uncle's mates might have brought the two of you together,' I said, while in the background a choir of children reprised their song of peace and love and the healing of wounds . . .

When the Specials were disbanded in 1970, after the Hunt Report had criticised their behaviour in the riots of August 1969 in Derry and Belfast, Jackie joined the full-time police reserve. He was stationed for a time in Ballynafeigh, next to the Red Lion on Belfast's Ormeau Road. Often in the evenings he would be on point duty outside the bar at the busy junction of the Ormeau Road and Sunnyside Street. This was on my father's route home to Finaghy from his work at the International Electronics factory – the 'Tab', as it was known – off the Castlereagh Road in the east of the city.* Jackie would always keep an eye out for the green Vauxhall Victor 'station wagon' (my father's English was still sprinkled with a pinch of Galt) and hold up the traffic to let his brother through.

One evening late in 1971 my father heard an explosion as he approached the top of the Ormeau Road, about five hundred yards from Sunnyside Street. He left his car in the middle of the road and joined the other motorists running towards the smoke that was billowing from the junction. The Provisional IRA had attempted to demolish the police station by leaving bombs in the premises on either side of it, a draper's shop and the Red Lion. The station was by sheer fluke largely undamaged (police stations were not then the fortresses that they were in later years), but the shop and the bar were wrecked, as was a bus that had been passing along the Ormeau Road in front of them. Through the dusk and the dust, in the rubble on the street, my father glimpsed a head of red hair: Jackie, he was sure, but in the moments before

---

* The Tab built computers, which in those days required the services of sheet-metal workers like my father. Nowadays most people would need a computer to find out what a sheet-metal worker was.

police officers pushed him back he realised he had been looking at the remains of a middle-aged woman. She was one of three people to die, blown out of the Red Lion's upstairs bar. The bombers had given all of ten seconds warning. The bomb went off after six. The woman didn't have a prayer.

My father was more than an hour and a half late getting home. We, of course, were frantic, news having reached us that a bomb had gone off when it had, where it had, and there having been no word from him. (Mobiles still science fiction, phone boxes frequently fucked.) He always came in from work by the back door. That night he could hardly make it through the kitchen. I will never forget him collapsing into the armchair just inside the living-room door, one hand shielding his eyes from us boys, or shielding us from them.

'I didn't know if it was a man or a woman,' was all he could say to my mother.

Jackie was one of those people for whom the Troubles had brought renewed purpose. Even as a child I think I was conscious that there was a lack in him, a yearning, although I would not have had the words then to describe it. My parents, watching him horse around with us boys, would say he was like a big kid himself. He had a great laugh, Jackie; he also had a very competitive streak. Football, Scalextric, running from one end of the garden to the other: there was no chance of Jackie ever *letting* you win.

When he married Molly Nobbs in the early 1950s he had bought a cottage in Knocknadona, a small townland several miles south-west of Lisburn. The cottage had no heating and no running water. It had a resident goat; it had (a source of horrified fascination for me and my brothers in later years) bottles jammed into holes all around the property to keep the rats at bay. It was exactly the kind of place that people in those days were moving into the new council estates to get out of. Now, as the Troubles got going in good and earnest, Jackie was in his early forties, childless (it would be far too simplistic to say that was his lack), and in a marriage that was beginning to fray at the edges, that would, in fact, in a very few years disintegrate completely. (The cottage, I don't think, can have helped.) He did not mind unsociable hours, or even dangerous postings. Eventually he was attached to the RUC's Special Patrol Group (SPG) in Armagh. The SPG had a bad reputation in the Nationalist community, a reputation that the SPG, and Jackie himself, seemed to revel in. Edmund, whose house in Portadown was only a few miles from the SPG's home base, answered a knock at his door one night to find Jackie, with a full SPG patrol parked out on the street behind him, offering his brother a case of 'liberated' whiskey. Edmund sent him on his way.

And yet Jackie was also very close to his cousin, Aggie's daughter, Eileen Hannon as was. Eileen had married Billy Lavery in 1955 – 'without lines', all her records having been lost in the burning of St Patrick's parochial house – but still lived in the cottage in Derrymacash to which she had been sent as an orphaned child of three.

(I was taken there a few times myself on family visits, although my brothers and I spent most of our time up the back field – you would have to call it – with Eileen's three sons, who at not much more than mid-teens any of them were driving a variety of clapped-out vehicles for our entertainment. While smoking.)

Midway between Portadown and Lurgan, Derrymacash had the name of being a strongly republican area. It was certainly

not an area where in the 1970s an RUC man – an *SPG* man –
would venture lightly without backup, or even with it. When
Billy Lavery died in 1972, however, Jackie attended the funeral
having just come off duty, with his uniform on under his
overcoat. Among the mourners were boys he recognised as
members of the IRA. They recognised him. They nodded to
one another across the grave. For today at least there was a truce.
Sometimes, the way Jackie told it, it all sounded like a bit of a
game – not the Michael Collins murder-go-round, not the
David Ervine serve-and-return; more like a grown-up cops and
robbers. Bang-bang, nobody's dead.*

It was Jackie who took Eileen on holiday to Plymouth, and
to meet their Uncle William's son Cecil, the time that Eileen
discovered that for one part of the Patterson family at any rate
she had never existed. This was a typical Jackie adventure. He
had called at Derrymacash one day with Eileen Smylie and
her son Jim in the car and told Eileen Lavery to pack a bag, he
was taking her away for a couple of days. And, yes, as I write
it, it does sound more like a well-intentioned arrest than an
invitation. None of his passengers had the first idea where
they were going, even when they boarded the ferry for
Stranraer. It is a bad enough drive down through England
from there when you know how far you still have ahead of
you. I can only imagine the despair in the car as the miles –
and miles, and miles – slipped past to Plymouth.

On other occasions he would drive Eileen to vigil mass at
St Patrick's in Derrymacash and, breaking every RUC safety

* This is not to trivialise the persistent rumours – some of them sub-
stantiated in court – that elements of the SPG in Armagh did actually
collude with loyalist paramilitaries in acts of terrorism, including murder, in
the 1970s.

guideline about predictable patterns of behaviour, return at the service's end to take her home again. In the climate of the times this was as risky for her as it was for him, but Eileen was not a woman who would be easily intimidated or dictated to. One photograph, taken on the jaunt to Plymouth, shows her linking arms on the one side with her new-found cousin Cecil and on the other with my cousin Jim, who holds up a poster displaying Jackie's mug-shot: 'Wanted, Dead or Alive, JP Supercop. Reward $3,000.'

No prizes for guessing who is on the other side of the camera.

In July 1974, the end of my first year at grammar school, I went to stay with friends whose father had just been posted to Derry as chief of the city's fire station. A couple of days after I arrived Jackie happened to phone my parents' house – probably around midnight, for Jackie's body clock was permanently on shifts, his dialling finger permanently itchy. When it came out in conversation with my father that I was in Derry, Jackie started to fret. He was there too, on an SPG posting. He wanted my father to give him the number of the people I was staying with so that he could talk to me and tell me not to let on to anyone that he was stationed in the city, and especially not to let on that he was stationed in the city with the SPG. My father talked him out of phoning. Glenn doesn't even know you are there to let on to anyone, he said. He was right. Neither did Glenn at that stage know what the SPG was or that his Uncle Jackie was in it.

The next morning Reserve Constable John Patterson phoned the fire station in Derry and, unable to speak to the chief officer directly, requested, as a matter of urgency, his home address. Then he drove, in full patrol again, to my hosts' house in the predominantly Protestant Waterside to tell me I was not to divulge to anyone that my uncle was there with his SPG unit. It was a Saturday. My friends' father had taken us on a day trip over the border to Donegal. After hanging about in the street for a few minutes, chatting to neighbours, Jackie and his colleagues drove back towards the city centre, taking the same detour they had taken on the outward journey, through the Waterside's main Nationalist estate, Gobnascale. A detour that had not gone unnoticed the first time by the local unit of the IRA, who had been busy in the interim mounting an opportunistic ambush. As the patrol drove past an embankment the gunmen hit it with rifle and machine-gun fire. The driver of Jackie's Land Rover momentarily lost control of the steering wheel and the vehicle went into a wild swerve. Jackie was pitched forward, which may have saved him from being hit square in the body by the bullets punching through the Land Rover's armoured plating but could not save him from the ricochet off the floor that entered his left buttock (or thigh, as the newspapers coyly reported) and lodged in his lower back.

It was late when we arrived back from Donegal. News of the shooting was conveyed to my friends' father while us children were getting ready for bed, but it was decided that it would be better to say nothing to me until the following morning. That afternoon my father collected me from the house and drove me to the nearby Altnagelvin Hospital. Jack was there, sitting by his wounded son's bed. As I came through the door of the isolation ward my Uncle Jackie smiled.

Belfast Telegraph, Monday, July 8, 1974   5

Policeman on patrol wounded

By Telegraph reporters

A POLICEMAN and several civilians were injured in weekend shooting incidents in Belfast and Londonderry.

A young Whitehouse man was seriously injured in an assassination attempt early yesterday and a 44-year-old Andersonstown woman was hurt when a bomb exploded in a man-hole near her home.

Incendiary devices damaged a pub and two chemist's shops in Londonderry and caused slight damage to a Downpatrick restaurant.

Belfast: A 20-year-old [...] was hit in the [...] jured when his patrol was fired on in the Strabane Old Road area.

Both chemist's shops were at Spencer Road in the Waterside district and the incendiary devices went off early yesterday morning. The first, severely damaged one of the shops but the [...] caused only [...] but did not hit him.

Ten shots were fired at an RUC patrol in the Strabane Old Road from the direction of Mistoox court. A policeman was hit in the thigh and taken to Altnagelvin Hospital, where his condition was stated this morning to be "comfortable".

which caused minor damage to La Bonne restaurant in Scotch Street.

Newry: Five high-velocity shots were fired over Eire at British troops on duty near the Forkhill Road manoeuvring route to Omeath but no one was h[...]

'Ah, there's the wee boy who got me shot,' he said.

I burst into tears.

'He knows I'm only joking,' Jackie said. 'Don't you?'

So needless to say I was still the Wee Boy Who Got Him Shot when I was leaving grammar school six years later.

Jackie had returned to duty in the interim, although never again with the SPG, and after various short-term postings had wound up at Lisburn Road police station on the main route into town from Finaghy and not far from my girlfriend's house. He would tell whoever was driving the Land Rover to stop any time he saw me, more often than not standing at the bus stop waiting for the last bus home. One night, for something to do, his colleagues set up a vehicle checkpoint while Jackie chatted to me until the bus came about how everyone was doing at home and me getting him shot and all that. Another night, seeing the Land Rover drawing up and not wanting to take any chances, I dumped in the bin bracketed to the bus stop the eighth of Red Leb I had bought earlier in the evening and had been nervously turning over in my pocket for the last ten minutes, never mind that there were rather more weighty, and lethal, Lebanese imports occupying the police's minds just then.* I went back the next morning, but no matter how much I tried to purposefully poke – 'Did I somehow contrive to drop my keys in here?' – I still looked like an out-and-out bin-hoker. I gave up: offered it up.

During the first emergency operation at Altnagelvin, the surgeons discovered that the bullet in Jackie's back had fragmented. (Bullets. Don't you just love them?) One or two of the fragments were so near the spinal cord that the surgeons agreed the least risky option was just to leave them where they were for now.

From the hospital Jackie had been transferred to the Northern Police Convalescent & Treatment Centre in Harrogate, North Yorkshire, where he became close for a time to one of his nurses. (I don't remember if 'close' is the word the family did use, but nor do I remember them saying anything less ambiguous.) Like I said, he had a great laugh, my Uncle Jackie, and a face-wide smile to go with it. Long after he had been officially passed fit to return to duty there were further spells in hospital – further failed attempts to get at the bullet fragments – followed by further spells in convalescent homes and, Jackie being Jackie, accompanied by further close friendships with convalescent-home nurses.

---

* A cargo of arms emanating from the PLO's Al Fatah section and destined for the IRA had been intercepted at Antwerp in 1977. (See PBS's Frontline Online website.) Lebanon, Libya, Spain, USA, Czechoslovakia, South Africa, even Norway . . . Northern Ireland has been a magnet down the years for tons upon tons of the world's less desirable metal objects.

All the while the cottage at Knocknadona was becoming more and more decrepit. I must have been about twenty the last time I was there. It is the paltriness of the light that sticks in my mind, which might account for my other, clearly unreliable, memory of the framed facsimile of the Covenant signed by my grandfather hanging on the wall.

For nights at a stretch Jackie was sleeping in the police station dormitory when he came off duty. So it was a relief as well as a surprise to the whole family when in the mid-eighties he married again — married a woman with no connection to the nursing profession, or the police, at all — and bought a large red-brick semi, a few hundred yards out the Hillsborough Road from Lisburn town centre, on a site overlooking the Lagan Valley Hospital. From the rear bedroom windows he could just about see the family plot in Lisburn cemetery. After all the years of overtime and unpopular shifts he was comfortably off, in fact he had more money nearly than he knew what to do with. He filled every room in the house with objects, often bought on a whim: Victorian china dolls, an amusement arcade's mechanical puppet show whose muteness he overcame by pressing 'play' on a hidden tape-recorder, so that the puppets jerked and twitched to the sound of Orange marching bands, blattering out the 'Sash' and 'Dolly's Brae'.

Call at the house any time of the night or day and you were likely to be asked would you take a drop of poitín with your tea. He did not drink much himself, poitín or anything else, in fact over the years he had had more than a passing acquaintance of his own with gospel halls. He just liked being able to produce the poitín bottle and tell you the story of its provenance (I could be as wrong about this as I was about the Covenant, but I think a friend of a friend of one of the Lavery boys may have featured), just as he enjoyed showing you the copies of *An Phoblacht*, the Sinn Fein newspaper, which he kept with his loyalist publications – *Beano* to their *Dandy* – under the living-room sofa.

After only a couple of years of the marriage his second wife walked out. Jackie was devastated. He had recently turned sixty and was facing compulsory retirement in two years' time. The job, though, was the least of what he would be losing. There was the camaraderie, the simple day-to-day contact.

He was also facing the prospect of yet another back operation, which was suddenly a cause of great distress. This one was to be performed in the Royal Victoria Hospital on the Falls Road, the IRA's Belfast heartland. As was routine in such circumstances, he would have a permanent police guard at the door of his private ward, but this did little to allay his fears. For the first time his superior officers expressed concerns about his mental health. Jackie had learned that they were going to ask him to surrender his personal-protection firearm, on the grounds that he was safer without it in his current state. He became even more anxious and upset. He claimed that the Provisionals had issued explicit and specific threats against him. There had been anonymous phone calls. They knew where he lived. Now, more than ever, he needed his gun.

And if his anxiety seems to border on paranoia it is worth remembering Ernest McCrum, shot dead on Antrim Street three years later, aged sixty-one and a few months off retirement. As with people in mixed marriages, your legitimacy as a target was greatly increased by the ease with which as a target you could be hit.

That summer, 1988, Jackie was admitted briefly to a psychiatric hospital. I was home from Manchester around this time, visiting my parents. My father brought Jackie to the house one day. My mother and I were sitting out in the back garden on deckchairs.

'There's the wee boy . . .' Jackie started to say when he saw me, and laughed like he didn't mean it, which he didn't, probably. He looked – and I hope I am capturing his demeanour here, not creating it in hindsight – chastened by his hospital experience. The word 'depression' would not have been given houseroom in 9 Antrim Street. 'Give yourself a shake,' Kate would have said. 'Get on with it.'

A member of the police welfare association called at his home on the afternoon of 10th August. Jackie seemed, in the light of his recent troubles, to be in very good spirits. The two of them chatted for a time over a cup of tea then Jackie saw his visitor to the door and almost as soon as he was alone went into the garage where he attached a hosepipe to his exhaust and fed it in through the passenger's side window. He stuffed the gap at the top of the window with old Christmas cards, saved perhaps with just such an end – such a dramatic contrast – in mind. Then he got into the car and turned the key in the ignition.

By the time he was found it was too late for the Lagan Valley across the street.

He was one of fifty-five officers of the RUC and full-time reserve to commit suicide between 1970 and 1996. He was one of only eight not to use his personal-protection weapon, which I suppose means that whoever had recommended taking Jackie's away had got something right.

I was already back in Manchester by this time. I received a
phone call that night when I got in from the pub. It was the
day after my twenty-seventh birthday. I had spent the
evening with my cousin Terry, Edmund's son, who lived
close to me in Rusholme in the south of the city. We flew
home together for the funeral on the 11th.

This was bang in the middle of the period when I was
thrashing around, trying to make headway with my second
novel (even the title was still a year off), set in a Northern
Ireland I was no longer confident that I knew. Jackie alone of
his brothers had not made it along to the Belfast launch of the
first novel back in March, the night that David informed me I
was a conduit for his ukulele stylings. To tell you the truth I
had not been entirely disappointed by his absence. You never
knew with Jackie. He could be charm itself or he could, as my
parents had said all those years before, be as disruptive as a
child. I was nervous enough without that added anxiety. My
novel, I grandly imagined, was a challenge to the orthodoxies
of Northern Irish politics and of Unionist politics in particular. Fortunately I had discovered in writing it that all
novels, no matter how challenging they fancy themselves, are
carried by characters who interact with or react against the
world around them. No one who read *Burning Your Own* ever
mentioned the word orthodoxies to me, but talked instead
about the Kid, the Dad, the Teenaged Cousins.

The trip back for Jackie's funeral, the enforced connect-
edness – community in its least political guise – that such
occasions inevitably bring, added to my belief that the only
way to solve the problems I was having with the new book
was to come back for longer. Which was, in a not altogether
roundabout way, how I came to be living in Lisburn twelve

months later, treating sick stories for the Arts Council of Northern Ireland and trying to dodge my Aunt Eileen's fifty pees in Bow Street Mall. It is only dawning on me now that Drew Linden in *Fat Lad* comes home for a funeral – his mother's – in advance of the longer return, for work, that makes up the bulk of the narrative. I am trying to work out if this was a conscious or an unconscious parallel or nothing more than a coincidence, because at this remove, nearly twenty years after I started writing it, I have difficulty enough remembering some of the characters' names.

Jump forward a novel, however, and Jackie is a definite presence:

Raymond adds the tale of a man he knew who lost his wife, and his house, in a fire and bought a million and one things with the insurance money trying to start again: a Parker Knoll chair, a three-piece suite in genuine leather, a bathroom suite in white and gold, two good beds for the two guest bedrooms, a Persian rug for the hall, an Afghan rug for the lounge, a picture for every wall, mirrors, plants, clocks galore, a 26″ colour television, a Betamax video recorder, the first of its kind, a VHS when Betamax's fortunes went into decline, a set of Waterford crystal glasses, six for red wine, six for white, six for whiskey, bottles of whiskey, bottles of wine, stacks of books from stacks of book clubs, a stack system hi-fi, every Ronco record, every K-tel compilation ever advertised, a Bontempi organ, a tuba on which he never got further than oom-pah-pah, oom-pah-pah, a whoopee cushion, just for a laugh, a dog to walk, a cat to stroke, dog and cat baskets, stuffed-snake draught excluders, gonks, ornaments, whatever caught his eye in Sunday colour

supplements – collectables and disposables, jewellery and
frippery – a week-by-week encyclopaedia of cookery, a
month-by-month encyclopaedia of everything else, a new
tool for his toolkit every fortnight, a wooden block containing The World's Sharpest Knives, by means of one of which,
when his life still refused to add up, he cut his throat,
reclining on the Parker Knoll chair, while clocks galore
struck twelve (his feet, convulsing, brought one crashing
down to stop, short, on the Afghan rug). He left a note.
Sorry, it said, I tried everything.*

I think in the end Jackie did.

---

* *Black Night at Big Thunder Mountain*, p. 143. Raymond is a labourer, and
former loyalist paramilitary, who along with German canteen worker Ilse
Klein is being held hostage on the Euro Disney building site by an
Imagineer named Sam. Well, it seemed like a good idea at the time I
was writing it. In truth there were days when I thought it was the best idea I
– *anybody* – had ever had. Which just goes to show.

Shorter, with Reverse Mood-swing

After Jackie's funeral the family congregated in my Aunt Eileen's house, just as we had done after Jack's funeral almost thirteen years before. He had died of a heart attack on 4th October 1975, a Saturday according to the Faith Mission diary's day-finding chart; the last of the children of Phares and Eleanor Patterson.* The day after, for the first football-season Sunday in three and a half years, the TV remained plugged-in in my parents' living room, opposite Jack's preferred armchair. The TV that made Kate titter and him tut. I would be amazed if my brothers and I did not switch on the *Big Match*. The death had felt rather remote from me, as indeed Jack had been in life. Three weeks later, to the day, my other grandfather, Billy, collapsed and died in Canada at the age of just sixty-five. He had visited Belfast the previous July, only the fourth time I had met him, and seemed to me wonderfully urbane with his smart sports

---

* The boys had died in the order that they were born, starting with William on Christmas Eve 1967. Even more curiously their ages at death decreased in sequence too. William and David both reached eighty-eight, Fred eighty-four. Jack, at only eighty-two, would eternally be the youngest.

jackets, his Rothmans cigarettes and his schooners of sherry. (He had hated the city he found on his return: pinched, mean-spirited; above all, even in high summer, cold. My mother had a hunch she would not see him back here.) I cried my eyes out when the phone call came then immediately felt bad that I had barely shed a tear over Jack.

Still, I had gone to my parents' bedroom early on the morning of his funeral to make sure I was going to be allowed to attend. It was not a foregone conclusion: until relatively recently women and children were positively discouraged at some Protestant funerals; and having built myself up to expect it I did not want to miss out on a day off school, as I had missed out on the occasion of Jamesie's funeral a few years earlier.

At the graveside a member of the Brethren told us to rejoice (one of a succession of Brethren members who detained us there in the cold as I recall it, no one in this particular fellowship being above another), rejoice, for Brother Jack had been found in an attitude of prayer. And I remember thinking – fourteen and new to scepticism – Brother Jack collapsed in the narrow space between the bed and the wall of his room in Eagle Terrace; the range of attitudes he might have been found in was severely circumscribed.

I am forty-seven now and no less sceptical, although I would hope I am nowhere near as cynical.

Eileen then was a few days past her sixtieth birthday, a few days into her official retirement, although I have no memory of her working at all after the move out of Antrim Street. (Before that she had worked in the canteen at Wallace High School.) She had always dreamed of retiring to Bangor: 'a wee house by the sea'; but here she was in Eagle Terrace no more than half a mile from where she was born. She might have been encouraged in her unfulfilled dream by the example of her relative by marriage, John Wylie, who had been living in the County Down resort for as long as my cousin Ella could remember, albeit living recently in a pensioner's bungalow on a housing estate off a ring road.* Eileen would take Ella there occasionally on visits, as my father would sometimes take Jack, and on one occasion took me, although my memory stops dead at the front of the house.

Ella had never heard the story of John Wylie's role in the riots of August 1920, but nor was she greatly surprised when I mentioned it to her. He was, she said, echoing something my father had told me, 'an angry wee man'.

After Jack's death, John Wylie suggested to Eileen that he and his wife Lizzie move into Eagle Terrace with her and Jim. There was more than enough room, and he wanted as he approached the end of his own life to come back home. Whether Eileen actually rebuffed him or just kept putting off a decision, he never did make it back. He died in Bangor not long afterwards. A few years later Eileen and Jim moved again (because John Wylie had been right, Eagle Terrace was too big for just the two of them) to a ground-floor maisonette on the Old Warren housing estate, built in the early sixties between the Longstone Road and the Hillsborough Road –

---

* The definitive Bangor novel is, in fact, *Ring Road* (Harper Perennial, 2004) by Ian Sansom, although his *Mobile Library* detective novels have, as the name suggests, roved a little further than his adopted town. Bangor is also home to Colin Bateman, Northern Ireland's most prolific novelist, and birthplace of Zane Radcliffe, no slouch himself. Which for a town of seventy-five thousand, whose last writers of note were the seventh-century monks responsible for the *Bangor Antiphoner*, is practically a Renaissance.

built, some of it, on land that Eileen's estranged grandmother had felt by right ought to be hers. Avonmore Street in Old Warren is the only trace that remains of the handsome and commodious lodge, ownership of which was to have proclaimed from its hilltop site that Phares and Eleanor Patterson, grocers, had well and truly arrived.

My Uncle David, who had picked up so much of Eleanor's story in particular on his rounds of Lisburn as a teenage trainee, worked his way up in the wholesale end of the grocery trade, becoming first manager of Thomas Crawford of Talbot Street in Belfast and in time owner. Later still he took over the firm of R. Christie and Co. in Newtownards, where he began trading as D. C. Patterson. His Uncle William, honouring the premises with a visit one day, not long before he died, looked admiringly at the new sign.

'I'm glad to see you have reinstated the Patterson name,' he said. 'We were a great business family.'

The name lasted until 1983 when D. C. Patterson merged with J. & J. Haslett Ltd, part of the Mace Group, who moved the business again, this time to Derriaghy, not far from the Orange Hall that Eddie Charley's niece opened in the days following the assassination of Archduke Franz Ferdinand. David's son Michael, who had joined the family firm from school in the mid-seventies, made the move too and in a very few years had risen to company director. When, early in the new century, Haslett's was in financial difficulties – was, in fact, in very real danger of going under – Michael and three of his fellow directors bought it over, although this time without a change of name. One of the employees whose jobs the buyout helped save was my brother Paul's daughter Lynn, who had in turn joined straight from school. The line may not have been exactly straight – Lynn worked in the wages department – but that was five generations of Pattersons in groceries.*

Talking of family names, there are no Eleanors in Lynn's generation and the only Phares, in Fred's line, is tucked away between two other forenames and a surname by marriage, which might well make the task of a future chronicler more difficult, even if digital information really is for ever and even if there is no late-twenty-first-century equivalent of the destruction of the Four Courts lying in wait, which we all, of course, in this new Ireland of mutually co-operating equals (Brethren, you might almost say), trust there is not.

Oddly, given the proliferation of site-specific memorials to the dead of the old Ireland of mutual loathing (see footnote p. 80), there is nothing to mark the exact spot outside the Northern Bank, now Shannon's Jewellers and Café, at the corner of Railway Street and Market Square, where Oswald Swanzy was shot. If you rewind the District Inspector's last steps, however, back inside the cathedral you will find on the north wall a brass plaque in an Irish oak surround put up by his mother and sister Irene:

In proud and loving memory of Oswald Swanzy DI Royal Irish Constabulary who gave his life in Lisburn on Sunday 22 August, 1920 and his gallant comrades who, like him, have been killed in the unfaltering discharge of their duty and in the service of their country. Be thou faithful unto death and I will give you a crown of life.

* Note the past tense. Lynn quit in 2007 for Spain, where she now sells time-share apartments and where she is, on reflection, a lot closer to the spirit of her great-great-grandparents than she was in the wages department of J. & J. Haslett Ltd.

Swanzy's mother survived only until 1922, but Irene was still placing *in memoriam* notices on the anniversary of her brother's death well into the 1970s. She had taken off around the world after her mother died, winding up in Fiji, where she met and married the Director of Public Works. Oswald's No. 1 dress uniform made the trip with her: don't ask me why. Genuinely, don't: I have not lost a brother, never mind in the circumstances that Irene lost hers. The uniform was eventually acquired by a collector in New Zealand from whom it was in turn acquired by the museum of Police Service of Northern Ireland, or PSNI; because of course the RUC has gone the way of the RIC before it.*

In the graveyard immediately outside the cathedral's south wall lies Louis Crommelin, who came to Lisburn to escape religious persecution, bringing with him his linen know-how and the key to the town's future prosperity. Stand with your back to his grave and you can see, off to the left, the rear window of the Linfield Bar, from which Peter McKeever was lowered, wrapped in a quilt, and, almost straight ahead, the window from which Mrs Gilmore, the owner of the sweet-shop, had to jump. And you think to yourself, why would anyone, even for twice the money they had ever handled, even for three times, come back after that?

---

* I am grateful to Billy Brown of the Northern Ireland Retired Police Officers Association for steering me towards the story of Irene and the No. 1 Dress Uniform. I met him for coffee one morning with a colleague whose mother had been a child in Lisburn in 1920: had carried with her all her life the vivid memory of Oswald Swanzy's polished shoes as he lay sprawled on the cathedral steps.

'Except,' I said, 'he died across the road from the cathedral.'

'Ah,' he said.

Like I'm one to talk about memory.

These buildings, tight against the perimeter of the cathedral, were among the first to be rebuilt after the fire of 1707. As for all that remains from before the fire, after decades of neglect (Charles Brett termed it a 'long-standing disgrace to the town'), Castle Gardens and its single Fulke Conway-era wall have recently been renovated and re-branded the heart of the new Historic Quarter, it being the fate of Lisburn as of so many of our towns and cities to be quartered for easier consumption. Actually it is all rather pleasant, right down to the obligatory glass-fronted visitors' centre. (Do architects not realise how much all this glass is devaluing those baby-stepping-into-the-light articles I used to write?) From the less ancient battlements at the highest point of the gardens you can look out, as the gamesters who frequented the fort here once looked out, south across the Lagan Valley, in the direction of Saintfield or, a shade to the west, Lisnastrain, Cargycreevy, Ballynahinch.

My cousin Sharon, David's daughter, has a house out this way. I understand that that is where the chiffonier now resides, although I am guessing with something other than soda bread in its super-centenarian drawers. Sharon's brother Michael is to the north of the town in Ballinderry. My own brother Paul is in Milltown, on the edge of Derriaghy, a mile and a half to the east. Of all of us cousins, Eileen's son Jim, up there in Old Warren, is the closest to the town centre, his route in taking him past the house on Chapel Hill where his mother spent her earliest years. Number 9 Antrim Street, where she lived between Eleanor's death and her own marriage, is no longer Apollo Window Blinds, but appropriately enough perhaps a branch of Money Shop, 'the UK's No. 1 for Cheque Cashing, Cash Advances (Cash 'til Payday) and Cash Loans'. (You get the idea OK? They deal in *cash*.) I

called in there one day and explained to the woman behind
the counter – and safety glass – what I was about and asked if
I could look around upstairs, maybe take a few photos. Her
colleague came out from what would have been Jack and
Kate's scullery, as I pointed out, thinking it might help prove
my bona fides. They looked at me as though I was the most
inept joint-caser ever, whereas of course in the film – the *caper*
– while I kept them distracted out front with the mumbling
and bumbling routine my accomplice, played by Lee Evans,
would have been in and out over the back wall with all the
Cash waiting to be Advanced 'til Payday. Which would be
wrong of Lee and me, I fully acknowledge.

The Australian woman working in the Cardan's bar and
grill – the Robin's Nest in my time on Bachelors Walk – was,
it has to be said, just as cautious to begin with, but after a
brief word with her manager told me to go ahead, snap away.
I snapped the chromey, leathery, cocktaily area to the right of
the main door, and the spruced-up, scrubbed-wood version of
a traditional Irish bar on the left, with its small library of
well-thumbed books: Grishams, Trollopes (J.), and Fieldings
(H.), the *Wine List* 2003, the Bible, but also Roddy Doyle
and David Park*, either of whom I would have loved to have
had at one of my literary evenings in the little-used upstairs
function room that now goes by the name of Distil nightclub.
(I would have taken Grisham, Trollope J. and Fielding H. as
well if they had agreed to the fee of fifty pounds and were able
to give proof of at least one Irish grandparent.)† All the same

---

* Another son of a Tab man.
† Charlton v. Kennedy: the rematch. In introducing the one-grandparent
rule Geordie Jack arguably did more to extend the notion of the Irish
diaspora than Camelot Jack ever did.

it is as hard, standing in front of the Cardan's bookcase, to imagine Desmond Hogan striding around the stage upstairs, reading – altogether too mild a word for what Desmond Hogan does with, to, from, a book – as it is to imagine a police inspector arguing out the window with an angry wee man on a crate.

Angry Wee Man, what would you make of Bibles in bars, punters swigging WKD blue as they discuss the relative merits of Exodus 21 and Matthew 5?

What would you make of Desmond Hogan?

At the other end of Bachelors Walk, across the junction with Antrim Street, Bow Street Mall has somehow swelled to twice the size it was when I moved back to Manchester at the end of 1991. Walking through it I feel a little of what I imagine my Aunt Eileen must have felt, as she sat on her bench in the middle of the Winemark–Stewart's–HMV triangle (the bench has vanished, Winemark has vanished, Stewart's is split between TK Maxx and Primark, HMV is elsewhere): a faint bemusement; wonder mixed with nostalgia. Or perhaps I flatter myself and misrepresent her: nostalgia? *Eileen?* After all that she had lived through?

The sequence is a little muddled in my mind, but bit by bit in the years after I quit Lisburn and the Arts Council post I became aware that certain things in the family tree my father's cousin Phares was researching were not adding up.

My mother, when I asked her at one point how it was coming along, had made vague mention of 'problems with dates', without letting on of course that she had known for the best part of twenty years exactly what lay at the root of those problems. She is like that, my mother, she will keep a secret for you. She will keep it, if you ask her, well after you and all belonging to you are dead.

It was only when I finally settled in Belfast with Ali, however, that I began to take any kind of sustained interest, and to try to work things out for myself. Maybe with all that was going on in my own life I had just become better at picking up the signals of other mixed marriages. Or maybe I am misremembering and it was my father who, faced with the newly established fact of Ali and me, wondered why he should remain tight-lipped any longer about his own mother's Catholicism. Or maybe it was a bit of both: I was about to knock when he opened the door.

All I know is we started to talk.

I was the one who found the marriage certificate that proved how long his parents had lived apart after his sister was born. (Why had I even gone looking there, ten years after they were assumed to have wed?) He was the one, with his story about John Wylie outside the Railway Hotel, who set me off looking into the Swanzy riots.*

When I read the newspaper report of the destruction of Mary Jane Logue's house, I said to him, 'This is a book.'

David didn't think so (my father is as bad with secrets as my mother is good), Edmund either, or so I gathered.

These were still uncertain times in Northern Ireland. Early on 12th July 1998 three young brothers, Richard, Mark and Jason Quinn had been murdered by loyalists who petrol-bombed their home on a housing estate in the County Antrim town of Ballymoney. Their mother, herself the child of a mixed marriage, was separated from the boys' Catholic

* I had never bothered much with the footnotes up till then.

father and living with her Protestant boyfriend. She was bringing her sons up as Protestants, had allowed them to spend the evening before they died out with their friends at the estate's 'Eleventh Night' bonfire.

Eight weeks after the referendum to ratify the Good Friday Agreement and the principle of power sharing it seemed we were still stuck in the Pentateuch, visiting unto the third and fourth generation the 'iniquity' of them that loved across the religious divide.

David didn't tell me to leave the past alone, he just let it be known that he would rather I didn't go disturbing it. And if I did insist on ignoring his wishes, I was not to expect any help from him.

I had no appetite for a fight, and no need of one: I had other books I wanted to write. I wrote two of them. I started a third.*

And then Eileen died.

She had amazed her carers in the Alzheimer's unit for almost a decade with her tenacity, repeatedly pulling through crises that would have put paid to a person in the prime of life. She even managed to recover her swallow. 'That's surely it now,' we said when we heard it was lost: the next most basic reflex after breathing; we said it half a dozen times more before the May day in 2004 when she finally slipped away. Her funeral two days later, the 12th, was my

---

* I also wrote a rare short story in which a radio producer is trying to make a documentary about his grandmother, who ran off to Canada (*Calgary*: you think I make nothing up?) in the 1920s, only to be thwarted by his great-aunt. 'It's not your story to tell,' she says.

'But Granny's dead. Who's left to tell it?'

'Who says you have to tell it at all?'

I believe the word is transference.

ninth wedding anniversary: a beautiful sunny Wednesday. Ali and I decided we might as well make a day of it and took the morning off work (a choice for me of turning left at the head of the stairs rather than carrying on straight towards my study). We had lunch in the garden before changing and driving out the back road to Lisburn.

The funeral home, on a corner at the town end of the Hillsborough Road, was a 1940s semi with pebbledash walls and a garage to the side converted into a neat, but featureless, chapel. Rearrange the stacking chairs in a circle and it would have passed muster with Jack as a meeting hall. Outside customised black-and-white traffic cones barred civilian cars from taking the hearse's parking space. Inside a baby monitor in a plug socket behind the lectern let the undertakers waiting in another part of the building follow the progress of the service.

Jackie had been buried from here too, the main road as well as the street up the side of the funeral home made almost impassable that day by the mourners. I will say this for the police here, whatever name they happen to be going by, they know how to see a colleague off; they have had enough practice down the years, I suppose.

Eileen's funeral was nothing like as large. She had been ill for such a long time, it was almost as though she had started to bow out a decade before. And then, too, she was a few months off eighty-nine. There were only so many people of her age surviving and fit to attend. My other grandmother, Annie, was there, returned from Canada since my grandfather died, so too was Eileen Lavery, looking frail and uncertain. Otherwise the majority of those taking their seats in the chapel were men and women in their sixties and seventies, like my father and mother, David and Edmund and their wives, or, like my brothers and I, spreading out into their forties.

The minister who conducted the short service was new to the parish. He had only met Eileen in the final stages of her illness, which is to say had never really met *Eileen* at all, and either did not have the time, or as yet the skill, to invest his second-hand knowledge of her with the spark of the person she had once been. She was, he said, sticking to the safe ground of observable fact, among the last of a generation, and I am afraid to say at that point my attention drifted for a time before settling again on the baby monitor. How odd, I was thinking: how very, very odd. Surely there was a better way of integrating a device of that kind into the surroundings, or customising it at least, like the black-and-white traffic cones out front. Even disguised as one of those awful plug-in air fresheners it would not have seemed so out of place, or such an unfortunate contrast with what I knew (and it was precious little then) about the beginnings of Eileen's life.

I was not listening closely enough to the service therefore to tell you the exact words that caused the undertakers to appear, as they appeared now, through a pair of sliding doors, and lifted the coffin from its bier before the minister. We followed them out, row by row – filings drawn to the magnet – and lined up on the street behind the hearse to walk the first few hundred yards towards her reunion with Jamesie in the cemetery at Blaris, about twice as far again out along the Hillsborough Road as the Lisburn Cemetery where her parents and brother lay. Her three remaining brothers took first lift of the coffin along with Ella's husband Wesley and I remembered again the day of Jackie's funeral and the moment when David, Edmund and my father had stepped forward to take his coffin from the pall-bearers and for the first time there were not enough Patterson boys to cover the four corners. I was never as aware as I was that day, receiving the tap on the shoulder to say it was the turn of my brothers and me to take our lift, that all of us were destined for the box too.

At some point on the walk behind Eileen's coffin I looked back over my shoulder towards the town centre, past Kwik Fit and the Fiat dealership (the new Lisburn Square facing, with Haslem's Lane unseen on the other side), to the gentle elbow bend, about where a Wallace Fountain once stood, connecting Bow Street to Chapel Hill. I would not call it a vision exactly, but I had a sudden powerful impression of a crowd massing intent on mayhem. (Oh, how they would have loved Kwik Fit: all those tyres; all that smoke!) I had a sense of a future in the balance, a future that had long since become all our pasts.

That phrase from the funeral service came back to me: 'the last of a generation'. Perhaps the problem was not the minister's but mine. It bore repeating after all. Soon there would not be a single person living who had witnessed the events that formed a backdrop to Eileen's life, and sometimes provided its central drama. Already the gaps were beginning to be glaring in the generation that came after. And as for my own generation, we had even less than the scraps our fathers and mothers had picked up. I turned again as the procession behind the hearse started to disperse. Before Ali and I had reached the car to drive the rest of the way to the cemetery, I had made up my mind I would write my book after all.

This time when I told my father it was out of politeness only.

'I don't think anyone's going to mind now anyway,' he said. The minister's words again, perhaps, or the weight of the coffin that could no longer be carried between the three of them.

Whatever, there I was all set to barge in if need be and there was the door opening again, wider than before.

I had been working on the book for over a year when my father suggested I call and see Eileen Lavery. She had been on my list of people to talk to, of course, but lodged firmly in my mind was the memory of how she had been at my Aunt Eileen's funeral. I was not a hundred per cent sure she had even recognised me when my father steered her over by the elbow to say hello. So it was more with a sense of nothing to lose than something to be gained that I drove with my father one late winter's day behind my Uncle Edmund's car and down the lane to Eileen's door: Eileen's new door. Well, new to me. The cottage she shared uneasily with Lizzie, lovingly with Tommy, is long gone. In its place stands a neat, modern bungalow, built for Eileen by her son Fergus, whose own house is in the next field over and connects to hers by a path through a gate in the hedge.

Eileen met us at the door, looking, on home ground, ten years younger than when I had last seen her, instead of a year and more older. She brought us through to the kitchen where teacups and cake (two types) were already laid out on the counter top and from the kitchen, when the tea was wet, into the living room, with its picture window framing a view across three townlands to the distant M1, a silent conveyor belt moving cars between Portadown to the right and Lisburn to the left. She talked the whole time. Talked, that is, when she wasn't listening to my questions and the supplementaries fired in from all sides by my father, my Uncle Edmund and my Aunt Isobel. This was the day she told me about the Patterson cold-shoulder and about Eleanor's little acts of kindness, the purple crocheted coat and the dress that was coveted even when it was a floor cloth. Whatever the impression given outside the funeral home (it's called shock, Glenn, and grief), there was nothing in the least the matter with Eileen's memory. What she could not tell me had not been lost: it had never been there to start with. So, no, she had not met my Aunt Eileen in Lisburn when they were both children, and, no, she had not heard anything either about the house on Chapel Hill and what befell it on the night of 23rd August 1920. In the course of the conversation, however, she mentioned as though it was some-thing I must already know, something moreover that was entirely in keeping with the man, that 'Uncle Jack' had hidden members of a Catholic family in the glory hole of 9 Antrim Street at the height of the rioting.

'Fusco,' she said. 'The ice-cream people.'

To which I fear I might have said that if there was one lot of people you would want to keep well away from the heat I supposed it would be ice-cream people. Because for a mo-ment or two I could not think what else to say.

Pietro Fusco had moved from southern Italy to Ireland in the opening decade of the last century, joining his brothers Alberto and Gaetano, who had wound up in Belfast by way of Black-burn. By 1920 Belfast had a well-established 'Little Italy' centred on York Street, running north out of the city centre. In Lisburn, however, the Italy could hardly have been littler, extending as it did not much further than the door out of Pietro's parlour on Cross Row, up by the cathedral gates.

From Cross Row to Antrim Street was little more than two minutes on foot, but it would have been a long, and an extremely hazardous, walk to attempt on 23rd August 1920 – the night that Fusco's was targeted – with the streets in between virtually abandoned by the police and army. Perhaps the flames, the inside-out pubs, the whole carnival of wantonness, provided just enough of a distraction for Pietro and his wife and their three sons to melt away. (I tried to avoid it, honest I did.) All the same, hiding in the glory hole suggests that the threat had by no means passed. If they had picked out 9 Antrim Street at random, in extremis, they were surely fortunate to find a refuge.* Instinct tells me, though, that there must have been some prior arrangement, or at least understanding: if it came to pass they would not be turned away; logic implies that any such understanding could only have been arrived at since some time the previous afternoon when the rioting broke out.

Either way – I will be honest here – it was only when the import of Eileen Lavery's words had percolated down that day in Derrymacash that I was able to feel for the first time

---

* Of all the 3,636 stories in the *Lost Lives* book by McKittrick et al., few are as nightmarish or as heartbreaking as the killing in August 1994 of Sean Monaghan, a twenty-year-old abducted by loyalists on the Lower Falls and taken to the neighbouring Shankill Road. Having somehow escaped from his captors he knocked on the door of a house whose elderly owner, recently returned from a church outing, phoned her daughter for advice. Her daughter came round with her boyfriend and took Sean Monaghan to her house, ostensibly to help him complete his escape. Instead he ended up back in the hands of the gang that had abducted him. He was shot four times in the head. This place, I tell you.

in a long, long while at all well disposed towards my grandfather.

Unlike some of his neighbours on Cross Row – the deeply traumatised Mrs Gilmore springs immediately to mind – Pietro Fusco did return to his business after the riots and in time opened a second parlour on the corner of Bow Street and Graham Gardens. In short, he thrived. When some years later a fellow Italian, the town's population having grown a little less little, lost his ice-cream parlour in a card game in St Joseph's Hall (had no one in Lisburn ever heard of playing for matchsticks?), Pietro came to the rescue and paid off the debt: memories maybe of his own past hardship, of the hand that had been extended to him.

His brother Alberto, who had a fish and chip shop in east Belfast, came through the riots there unscathed, but in the next serious sectarian outbreak in the city, in 1935, he got wind of a plot to burn him out and moved his family to Beechmount in the west. Such is the haphazardness of hatred, however, or the indomitableness of the entrepreneurial spirit, or just the appetite for good ice-cream, that another scion of the Fusco family, a son of brother Gaetano, was able eventually to make the return journey, opening a parlour on the Woodstock Road.* Ali and I would go there the odd time when we first moved to that side of town, the year of our

* My father told me the story of the card game in St Joseph's, which had passed into Lisburn lore. For the rest of the Fusco family history I am indebted to Angelo Fusco, grandson of Alberto, the fish-and-chip Fusco. Now in his seventies Angelo is still filleting fish in Bishop's on Bradbury Place, close to Queen's University. If I were Bishop's I would advertise this in my big front window. I would have Angelo there in the window, filleting away, where everyone could see him: 'Our fast food has been a hundred years in the making . . .'

wedding, the year after the ceasefires that signalled the beginning of the end of the last of the twentieth century's Troubles. We turned right as we came out of the door to head for home. Had we turned left and carried on a couple of hundred yards we would have arrived at the address where Eleanor was (said to be) living when she married Joseph Kelso Davis a century before.

I was on the point of writing that I doubt she would have approved of us, but then until I visited Eileen Lavery I would have doubted she would have approved of her youngest son hiding Catholics in the glory hole.

What am I saying, 'approved of'? 'Assisted', why not? She lived there too.

At which point I reflect that Fusco's ice-cream parlour was attacked earlier on the evening of the assault on Chapel Hill. Maybe Pietro and his family were not the only people sheltering in Antrim Street that night. Maybe the answer to the question of what happened to Kate and Eileen is, after all, the one you would have hoped at the beginning was the most obvious – the only possible – answer: even if it was for just one night, just this once, they were taken into the house that would eventually become their home.

It was around the time that I was grappling with this that I reached page 213 of Philip Roth's *The Human Stain*, from which I have taken one of the epigraphs for this book. 'Now that they're dead,' the passage runs in full, 'nobody can know. For better or worse I can only do what everyone does who thinks that they know. I imagine. I am forced to imagine. It happens to be what I do for a living. It is my job.'

Nathan Zuckerman, Roth's writer-narrator, is every inch the fiction that Coleman Silk and Faunia Farley are, the lovers whose private lives he must reconstruct in the wake of (if you don't want to know the result, look away now . . .) their murder by Faunia's estranged husband. His words, though, are no less truthful and pertinent for that.

And yet, as much as they function as characters in a story, Jack and Kate were my grandparents. They were as real as I am, as you are. (Tell me you are.) It is one thing to imagine a post-coital glow for them (that's *my* job?), but no matter how elusive they are there are facts, things that happened once in one way only. To get at them it is sometimes easier to start at the other end, with what you cannot imagine.

It has remained in the balance for me all the while I have been writing this book, but knowing what I know about the Fuscos, I just cannot imagine that Jack, with or without his mother's approval, would have left Kate and Eileen's fate to chance while Lisburn burned.

Epilogue

In his *Topographical & Historical Account of Lisburn* written in 1834 Henry Bayly refers to an 'unusual and wonderful' echo identified half a century before by a man named Hale in the appendix to his Work on Sounds. Hale had left detailed directions to its precise location, in Latin. Working off his own translation Bayly set out to find it, but without success.

'It is supposed,' Bayly wrote, 'by the various alterations which have lately been made in the town, the Echo is lost.'*

Half a century on again, though, in August 1887, the *Northern Whig* newspaper located the echo – 'one of the most extraordinary in the kingdom' – in the vicinity of Wallace Park, at that time just recently laid out and railed in according to Sir Richard's instructions. Again the deterioration of the effect was noted and put down to development, not least the coming of the railway, which skirted Lambeg and Hilden to enter the town along the western side of the

* I have read Bayly's translation and, never mind the echo, *I* was lost after the first sentence.

park. But while the echo's full wonderful character might have been diminished the *Whig* was keen to impress upon its readers what a remarkable phenomenon it remained:

> The whistle from the up-trains of the Great Northern, and the heavy rumble of the steam engine and the carriages, as they pass along the tunnel-like edge of the Wallace Park towards the Lisburn station, may be heard echoing from a bridge half a mile away, and as if the sounds indicated the approach of a train coming down from Moira.

For all the talk of development Lisburn was then still no more than a good-sized market town, compact and with clearly defined limits. Today it is a city by aggregation – or if you want to be pedantic a city by virtue of its success in the 2002 Queen Elizabeth II Golden Jubilee City Status Competition: the familiar twenty-first-century mess of orbital, inner ring, omniplex and retail park, and housing estate after housing estate after housing estate; incommodious, not a few of them, and seldom very handsome.

Wallace Park, on the other hand, remains much as it was in 1887. The original railings were sawn off at the start of the Second World War (the stubs are still visible) and have only recently been replaced by black spears, bought, it appears, job-lot from the set of a film about a much earlier, sword-and-sandals dust-up; but the low, greystone wall underneath, fronting the Belfast Road, is in better nick than most buildings half its age elsewhere in the town. (You wouldn't be surprised if the fella that built it came walking round the corner to check the mortar was dry.)

Just past the park gates the Belfast Road forks on to the Belsize Road, along which Oswald Swanzy's killers made their escape in Sean Leonard's taxi. (How did he think he *wouldn't* be caught?) Eagle Terrace is a short walk away, across the road and back towards the town then down the steps at the side of the Methodist Church on to Wesley Street and the Low Road. Long before he moved here Jack was a frequent visitor to the park. There was (is still) another entrance on the Magheralave Road, just behind the Railway Street courthouse, a couple of minutes from Antrim Street. During the war Jack had an allotment up at the Belfast Road end, where in my teenage years, the allotments having reverted to their original sporting purpose, I turned out (and sometimes not much more) for Lisburn Youth Football Club. Occasionally we played our matches on a pitch, closer to the Magheralave Road, nestling at the bottom of steep tarmac embankments. In the late 1940s Lisburn had experienced something of a cycling craze. Huge crowds would come from far and wide to watch top cyclists compete on the park's old, flat, cinder track. The new, banked track was built to attract even more high-profile events. It didn't. None of the locals could get round the new track without risk to their lives. The craze passed. The track fell into disrepair.

In between the allotment pitches and the cycle-track pitch is Lisburn Cricket Club, founded in 1836 and the oldest in the north of Ireland.* Wallace Park was practically

* I am reminded of a documentary I worked on in the mid-1990s called *Baseball in Irish History*. At the time there was only one baseball team in Belfast (we filmed them playing among – definitely 'among' – themselves), yet the sports shops were selling enough bats to equip an entire major league: or, indeed, a major terrorist organisation, which was observing the letter and not the spirit of its ceasefire by beating the fuck out of alleged joyriders rather than, as it had hitherto, shooting off their kneecaps.

landscaped around the club's existing pitch. Jack was a lifelong fan, often spending entire summer Saturdays at the park, walking back to Antrim Street for the lunch and tea intervals. If I close my eyes I can almost convince myself that I remember sitting beside him on the white-painted benches outside the pavilion, can remember even the sound of bat-on-ball carrying to us from the centre of the pitch; as if there was anything in the least exceptional about such a memory (the distillation of a score of toffee ads), or such a sound (the essence almost of the game itself).

That is the problem with memory: it is so susceptible, gullible, even.

During the entire two-year period when I lived and worked in Lisburn I do not recall once setting foot in Wallace Park. As a man in his late twenties my fear of public parks was at its height – maximum visibility, minimum cover; and anyway, in order to reach the park by the nearest, Magher-alave Road, entrance I had to pass the train station, which, frankly, with Belfast and all my friends ten minutes up the track, I lacked the will to do.

Two decades on I am a born-again park-goer (alas, Jack, as born again as I am ever going to get), the father of two young girls who know no fear, who look at all that greenery, those swings and slides and climbing frames, that mad cycle-track I wouldn't be surprised, and see only possibility. Even when I am on my own now I carry with me into wide-open spaces, like a bag of antiseptic wipes, something of the immunity of my children: *I have a right to this . . .*

Wallace Park was always last on my list of Lisburn locations to revisit. I arrived there early one Saturday after-noon in June at the end of a long circuit that had taken in my old flat, the Mall, the Fairy Mount, Merchants' Row, Smith-field and the view from Castle Gardens. Unfortunately I had managed to pick the day of the Lord Mayor's show, so that the park was full of vintage sports cars and fairground rides and some local radio presenter kidding himself he was a DJ. (Here's a clue, guy, it's not how *loud* you say it . . .)

I wandered around for half an hour trying to work out at what point reverberation ended and echo began, trying too to identify the most likely places from which to conduct my own experiment. I discovered a flight of steps – two dozen, my calves said – or re-discovered them, because when I reached the top and saw the duck pond I remembered having been brought up here as a child. I turned and looked out across the park. A train passed in the cutting beyond the cricket pitch. If it whistled at all the sound was drowned by the music and the DJ's repartee and the shrieks from the waltzer and the chair-o-planes. Still, I thought I knew where to begin. I decided to come back some day when it was less busy.

Then it rained for a month.

By the time the rain stopped – it was a Saturday morning and suddenly very, very quiet – I had four days to finish a draft of the book. Ali was away on a week-long work trip. My parents, who might otherwise have babysat, were at a wedding. I packed a picnic in a hamper retrieved from the attic, got the two girls and one buggy into the car and headed out to Lisburn before the clouds had a chance to regroup. En route I told Jessica, the elder at five, that I wanted her to help me with something for my book. I explained that we were on the trail of a Mysterious Lost Echo.

'Like *Scooby Doo*,' she said.

'A bit.'

'Who do you want to be?' she asked.

The cricket club was at home that day. The match was in its opening stages as we came through the gates, only twenty-four runs on the board; only half a dozen spectators outside the pavilion. The rain overtook us, travelling in a nothing-looking cloud, before we were halfway towards the duck pond. We ran for shelter to the bandstand where we played Noah's Ark, with Jessica as the dove, darting in and out to see if it was safe yet to emerge (she had had nearly the full forty days and forty nights in which to practise), and Miranda, a couple of days shy of eighteen months, as Mrs Noah, running in circles and shouting, as anyone would after being cooped up with their family, and never mind the other animals, for all that time. We even contemplated having the picnic right there,* ignoring the graffiti and the little patches of ground-in glass, until Mrs Noah needed changed and the dove said come to think of it she could do with going too, and so we had to traipse back to the toilets next to the gates we had come in by and start all over again.

There were maybe two more runs on the board, a couple fewer spectators in the stand.

We had our picnic eventually and came at the ducks by an upper path, to save me having to haul the buggy and our oversized hamper (I think the model name might actually be

* Here speaks a veteran of the Majestic Picture House's Saturday Morning Club: Cliff and the Shadows – Melvyn Hayes! No venue too unpromising, no setback too great to stop us, kids: let's do our thing right here, right now! It was bombed, the Majestic. Every Saturday Morning Club on the Lisburn Road was bombed.

the 'Brideshead') up twenty-four concrete steps. A guy was sitting on one of the benches at the side of the pond, eating lunch with a plastic fork. He had his shoes off, his feet resting on top, as though he had walked a very long way to get there. He asked me the time as I passed. Russian. I stood with the girls at the top of the steps, and this time all I could see was foliage. All that rain we had had. It was hard to imagine our voices carrying to the far side of these trees, never mind the park. And besides when I had thought about this moment as we were driving out here I had imagined there just being the three of us, without the audience (audi*ent*?) finishing his Spar pasta salad behind us.

'Come on,' I said, 'we'll go down to the swings.'

An hour later I was flagging. The rain had held off, had given way in fact to warm sunshine, and the park had been steadily filling with people while we had been there, a number of them the late-teens carry-out brigade (those telltale bags in off-licence blue) who had turned me off parks in the first place. It had been a long week with Ali away. I was for going back to the car and crossing my fingers for one more rain-free day when I could return alone. Jessica – Velma to my Shaggy – was appalled that we were giving up without solving our mystery, although it has to be said there was an element in this of just not wanting to leave the park. I let her run to various bits of higher ground down around the Magheralave Road gates, trying to convince herself she had heard something coming back from her shouts. (I had always thought that my eldest daughter had a loud voice, but sitting on a bench watching her thirty feet away cup her hands around her mouth and practically levitate with effort, I realised it was a tiny, tiny thing.) Then she suggested we ask someone. I explained to her again with the infinite patience of fatherhood that the whole reason we were doing this was because it was a *lost* echo. No one knew any more where it had been, or even that it had been there. To illustrate my point I asked the next likely-looking (that is, elderly) passer-by.

'Excuse me, are you from Lisburn? Did anyone ever tell you about an echo that you used to be able to hear somewhere in the park?'

The man pointed back over his shoulder towards the duck pond.

'There was a man,' he said, 'used to walk up around there and whistle. You would hear it echo all over the park if you were sitting watching the cricket.'

Jessica did me the kindness of not meeting my eye when she hummed.

In mitigation I should say that the next four elderly people we asked (two couples) had no idea what we were talking about – the whistler any more than the echo – even though they were Lisburn born and reared too and in the case of one couple, pushing their grandson in his pram, had been coming to the park two or three times a week for more years than they cared to remember. But back up towards the duck pond we went anyway. The Russian guy was still on the bench, feet resting on his shoes, but sparked right out now, asleep. With my back to him I whistled the only tune I could remember all of a sudden, 'A Message to You, Rudy'. (Well, my uncle was in the Specials.) Miranda danced in circles this time, clapping her hands. Jessica, who of late had been practising her whistle the way some children practise the piano, and with the same heartbreaking lack of progress, joined in with the words: 'Better think of your future, else you'll wind up in jail.' (It is one of my default-setting songs, as a friend's father calls them. I fear it is now one of Jess's.) '*Rudy . . .*'

Almost at once a female voice could be heard from the trees to our left, 'Rudy!' A dog – some make of terrier – checked its run and scampered back towards a woman stepping out from a stand of trees. When she drew level with us a minute or two later, I called across to her. 'Is your dog called Rudy? Only . . .'

'Trudy,' she said firmly, keen I thought to put a bit of distance between her and us.

She would have been even keener a few seconds later when I gave up on the whistling altogether.

I had discussed with Jessica in advance what we would shout. I wasn't just looking for an echo: I wanted my big yell to be directed at my grandparents, over the heads of everyone else in the park. We had talked about their names, pure and simple. Given the recent trends in forenames, however, if I had shouted Jack and Kate I would have had half the under-tens in Wallace Park running towards me, or, given other recent trends, half the parents of under-tens. Besides it had to be something all three of us could manage, which narrowed it down considerably. 'Hello' was an obvious contender and, as of that very day, 'so' had come into the frame too, Miranda having apparently cottoned on that all that was required to kick-start a conversation was this one word and an averagely self-absorbed interlocutor. (She had mastered 'wow' as well, which would be useful to throw in here and there to the monologue that would inevitably follow.) What we had settled on, however, was Miranda's first ever approximation of speech:

'Thank you.'

For the mess of it all, for your frailty as well as your moments of courage, for your inconsistency as well as your capacity for forgiveness, for your watch chains, your diaries, your jumble-sale hats, your haggling over flutes and fruit, your heads full of fairies and free-form prayer, your dreaming you dwelt in marbled halls and your mansion in the sky, for meeting when and how you did (whenever and however, that is, you did), for being helpless in the face of love and desire, for getting there eventually, for getting us here, shouting at you.

'Thank you.'

We turned and aimed it in all directions. The woman walking Trudy the dog glanced over her shoulder at us. The teenagers with the blue bags peeked out from their base in the bandstand at us. The couple with their grandson dragged their eyes away from his pram for a moment. A group of tourists on the path below us stopped and stared. The Russian guy on the bench by the duck pond woke up. (Sorry again, Russian guy.)

We weren't really getting anywhere, I knew: we could have sneezed and all of those people would have been close enough to say 'bless you' (or '*s Bogom*', I suppose); but to be standing up on a hill like that, shouting at the top of our voices had come to seem like an end in itself. Miranda had got in on the act too, bending over for greater force. Jessica, following my lead, had added a couple of words to the chant:

'Thank you, *Man*! Thank you, *Woman*!'

I picked both girls up in my arms and told them, when I counted them in, to give it everything they had.

One, two, three . . . I held my tongue as they let rip their thank yous.

And do you know, they are echoing in my head still.

In memoriam J & K, up a tree for ever

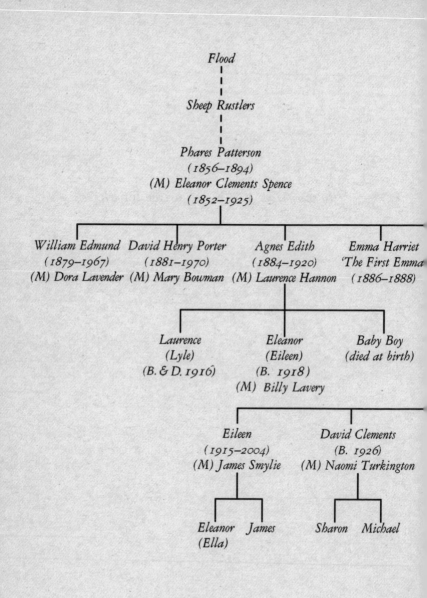

Flood
┊
Sheep Rustlers
┊
Phares Patterson
(1856–1894)
(M) Eleanor Clements Spence
(1852–1925)

William Edmund
(1879–1967)
(M) Dora Lavender

David Henry Porter
(1881–1970)
(M) Mary Bowman

Agnes Edith
(1884–1920)
(M) Laurence Hannon

Emma Harriet
'The First Emma
(1886–1888)

Laurence
(Lyle)
(B. & D. 1916)

Eleanor
(Eileen)
(B. 1918)
(M) Billy Lavery

Baby Boy
(died at birth)

Eileen
(1915–2004)
(M) James Smylie

David Clements
(B. 1926)
(M) Naomi Turkington

Eleanor   James
(Ella)

Sharon   Michael

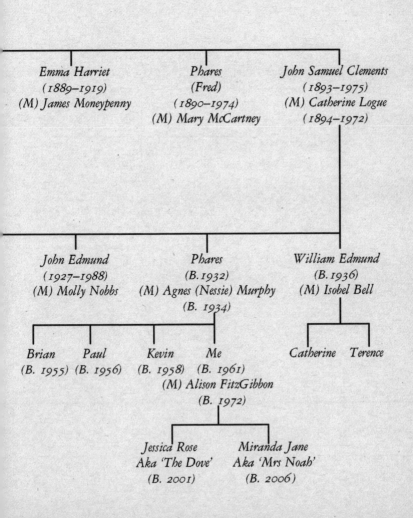

Emma Harriet
(1889–1919)
(M) James Moneypenny

Phares
(Fred)
(1890–1974)
(M) Mary McCartney

John Samuel Clements
(1893–1975)
(M) Catherine Logue
(1894–1972)

John Edmund
(1927–1988)
(M) Molly Nobbs

Phares
(B. 1932)
(M) Agnes (Nessie) Murphy
(B. 1934)

William Edmund
(B. 1936)
(M) Isobel Bell

Brian
(B. 1955)

Paul
(B. 1956)

Kevin
(B. 1958)

Me
(B. 1961)
(M) Alison FitzGibbon
(B. 1972)

Catherine   Terence

Jessica Rose
Aka 'The Dove'
(B. 2001)

Miranda Jane
Aka 'Mrs Noah'
(B. 2006)

Acknowledgements

Thanks first and foremost to my father and mother, Phares and Nessie Patterson, for the hours and hours and hours they gave up to this, and apologies if at times it all seemed a bit Stranraer-to-Plymouth without the road signs; thanks, in the same vein, to David and Naomi Patterson, to Edmund and Isobel Patterson, to Ella McCamley, to Eileen Lavery, and to Emelie and Ger FitzGibbon. Thanks too to Caroline Magennis, who assisted in the research (the cheeses! Isabella P. Dunwoody!), and to the Queen's University Belfast Publications Fund for paying me to pay her. Thanks to Brenda Collins at the Irish Linen Centre and Lisburn Museum, to William Roulston at the Ulster Historical Foundation and to everyone at the Public Records Office of Northern Ireland. Thanks to Colin Montgomery at Ellis Law Searchers (which I still refuse to accept is not a lost John Wayne film), to Billy Brown, Joe Kelly, John McKenna and Angelo Fusco. Thanks, by no means leastly, to Jessica and Miranda for their big, big shout, and to Ali for much more than I can possibly say.

And to your man who never wrote back to my very polite (I thought) letter: my nose still has the same amount of skin on it.

A NOTE ON THE TYPE

Linotype Garamond Three – based on seventeenth-century copies of Claude Garamond's types, cut by Jean Jannon. This version was designed for American Type Founders in 1917 by Morris Fuller Benton and Thomas Maitland Cleland, and was adapted for mechanical composition by Linotype in 1936.